# Audrey Hepburn in Paris

MEGHAN FRIEDLANDER

FOREWORD BY GIAMBATTISTA VALLI

INTRODUCTION BY LUCA DOTTI

HARVEST

*An Imprint of* WILLIAM MORROW

# CONTENTS

FOREWORD BY GIAMBATTISTA VALLI
5

INTRODUCTION BY LUCA DOTTI
6

{1} MEETING COLETTE
9

{2} *SABRINA*
17

{3} THREE DAYS IN PARIS
27

{4} *FUNNY FACE*
35

{5} HÔTEL RAPHAËL
47

{6} *LOVE IN THE AFTERNOON*
51

{7} MR. FAMOUS AND ASSAM
61

{8} PARIS FASHION WEEK
65

{9} *HARPER'S BAZAAR*—
PARIS PURSUIT
73

{10} LE BAL DES PETITS LITS BLANCS
83

{11} *PARIS WHEN IT SIZZLES*
89

{12} COCKTAILS ON THE SEINE
97

{13} *THE LONGEST DAY* PREMIERE
101

{14} *CHARADE*
107

{15} *VOGUE*—THE GIVENCHY IDEA
117

{16} *MY FAIR LADY* PREMIERE
125

{17} *HOW TO STEAL A MILLION*
133

{18} *TWO FOR THE ROAD*
145

{19} SOIREES AT THE ROTHSCHILDS'
157

{20} *BLOODLINE*
165

{21} OSCARS DE LA MODE AND
GALA SIDA À PARIS
173

{22} L'ORDRE DES ARTS ET
DES LETTRES
179

{23} *GARDENS OF THE WORLD*
AND UNICEF
185

{24} GIVENCHY'S FORTIETH
ANNIVERSARY RETROSPECTIVE
193

{25} AU REVOIR, PARIS
200

ACKNOWLEDGMENTS
202

PHOTO CREDITS
203

NOTES
204

# FOREWORD

DEAR AUDREY,

I'm sitting by the swimming pool at the Beverly Hills Hotel having my breakfast before taking the plane back to Paris, and everything that surrounds me makes me think of you. This delicate nature, so fragile and strong; this balance in the imbalance; this predominant pink, so tender but so determined, so steady, so touching in essence and spirit. I think of a Paris that I have conquered as you have conquered, a Paris that from this heat and this harmony leads us to introspection, to the essence, Paris takes you to an "editing" of all this fragility, of all this beauty that now encircles us.

Since I arrived in Paris, I have always had an obsession, a positive obsession, an image of you with your great friend Hubert in a private conversation that I perceive as the foundation of life. This image of you walking on this infinite, interminable dock, in a moment suspended in time in which there is neither past nor future, something that is immortalized in the present moment for the next centuries, a moment of extraordinary intimacy. In this moment you are this "essence," this mixture of fragility and extraordinary strength, this femininity, and this virility, almost an androgyny, which was and still is my obsession, and possibly of the rest of the world as well. This is the image that has always supported me when Paris lacks that kind of sun, that warmth, that kind of nature, that pink hue, this is the image that warms me at all times, a *point de repère*, an emergency exit in the coldest moments, in those with too many clouds.

I've always loved the idea of your personality, adaptable and peculiar. There is an Audrey in Rome, an Audrey in Beverly Hills, and there is an Audrey in Paris, where you become the Audrey of *Funny Face*; you conquer the catwalks, the couturiers, the photographers, the unforgettable images of bistros and Parisian counters, but you always remain true to yourself. This naturalness of yours in entering the culture of another while managing to remain totally intact is the most extraordinary thing.

I've always liked this "editing" in which France has been modernized thanks to your silhouette, thanks to your Hubert de Givenchy or your Courreges, all those images that are still attached to my board, like on that of all the designers of my generation. On our walls there is always a photo of you, a photo of you in Paris, in this "Ville Lumiere" where you brought your light, a light that shines.

—GIAMBATTISTA VALLI

---

PREVIOUS PAGE Audrey at the Orly Paris Airport, Paris, France, 1962. OPPOSITE Audrey at a cocktail party for *Breakfast at Tiffany's* in Paris, France, 1962.

5

# INTRODUCTION

## LUCA DOTTI

*To be ignorant of what occurred
before you were born is to remain always a child.*

—MARCUS TULLIUS CICERO

My mother, the Audrey Hepburn I grew up with, was far more interested in listening to the day-to-day dramas her family provided than gushing over her own glory. After she passed away, isolating myself from her public life steadily became my way to heal, or at least bury part of the pain.

My wake-up call came in the form of a surprisingly strong letter from one of Mum's best friends, Hubert de Givenchy. In the letter he urged me to understand that out there lived another Audrey, one who mattered to the world that adored her, and one I could not ignore. If you have ever pulled a thorn from a child's foot, you know exactly how his words felt. First there was an initial rush of pain followed by anger, then rejection, which was very slowly replaced by solace, and finally gratitude.

Removing that thorn led to an appetite for knowledge and the discovery of a genuine and seemingly infinite source of wisdom: Audrey Hepburn's fans. They became my guides, helping me bridge the gaps between my memories and history.

*Audrey at Home*, my first book with Harper-Collins, was effectively a way to cross that bridge, blending personal memories, recipes, and familiar locations, with just a zest of stardust and glamour. But one place weighed heavily for its silence: Paris.

Its exclusion wasn't intentional, nor was it negligence. The reason is quite straightforward; *Audrey at Home* was about the places my family called home during our lives together, and Paris was not one of them. Mum's story in the French capital largely predated my life and was strongly attached to her film career.

Most didn't notice this snub, and there wasn't a follow-up letter from Hubert. (To the contrary, one recipe from *Audrey at Home*, boeuf à la cuillère, did create a path of a newly found friendship.)

Yet some others obviously did notice. While the French, and in particular the Parisians, seldom are moody, here they had an extra reason to be "très ennuyés." Half of my mum's career revolved around Paris: her look, her best friends (to say nothing of her Yorkshires) were all fiercely Parisians, and still, she refused to call Paris "home"? But this dichotomy is apparent, for you see, the real Audrey Hepburn was part of that Hollywood gang who dined at home, who went to bed early, and who drew an unconditional line between the public and the private self. In other words, she was just as happy in a pair of jeans as in a Givenchy. *Audrey at Home* shared the former but now it is time to explore the latter.

Inevitably, time is central to this story. It always is, or at least as much as Jacques de La Palice is

French. While writing this introduction the world is frightfully close to yet another global war, we are still battling the worst pandemic in a century, and inflation and climate change are clear and present dangers. Maybe then, it's not the best time to dive into the past, through five decades of joie de vivre? Or, maybe, quite the contrary.

If you look closely, Audrey's world was ours through the looking glass. World War II was just over, the one against polio ongoing. The world was in the process of being rebuilt, and while many had lost everything, they still dreamed. Audrey's personal story, her movies, her fashion, her Paris are just about that, not losing faith in the future.

Our Cicero in this travel through an extraordinary time, Meghan Friedlander, is quite "extraordinaire" herself. Well known to Audrey's fans under the name *Rare Audrey Hepburn*, she is as unique as the photos and stories she publishes online. The very idea of this book is built around her; she has both the knowledge and the determination to plunge into Paris's rabbit hole and emerge from it with impeccable "chic." Better than that, our unique reporter has abided by the first time-traveler's rule, which is to set a date and end up somewhere completely unforeseen, as most of the stories you will find here were previously untold.

Ladies and gentlemen, please fasten your fashionable seat belts to discover Meghan Friedlander's account of Audrey in Paris. ✳

---

ABOVE Audrey at Givenchy's atelier in Paris, 1956.

# 1

# Meeting Colette

Nineteen fifty-one was a pivotal year for Audrey Hepburn. The twenty-two-year-old actress had signed with the Associated British Pictures Corporation (ABPC) and was gradually earning small roles in British films. Behind her were the exhausting days of rushing around London performing as a chorus girl in nightly musical revues. She was now gaining a reputation as a young starlet with considerable promise. There were many exciting ventures on the horizon, but one in particular would launch Audrey's career and introduce her to Paris for the first time.

In April of 1951, Audrey accepted a role in Jean Boyer's upcoming movie, *Nous irons à Monte Carlo* (*We Will Go to Monte Carlo*), which was scheduled to film in Monte Carlo that summer. This was Audrey's first substantial role; however, the offer presented concerns for the inexperienced actress. Having worked nonstop since the end of World War II, Audrey had become the main breadwinner in her household, and accepting a job abroad could hinder potential work opportunities back home in London. Despite her hesitations, she desperately needed the money and production offered to pay for her mother, Baroness Ella van Heemstra, to accompany Audrey to Monaco.

Better yet, the studio promised that her character would wear a Dior gown. As an impassioned admirer of French fashions, Audrey was delighted at the prospect of wearing a true couture design. There

was one final condition: the movie was to be filmed twice, once in French (*Nous irons à Monte Carlo*) and again in English (where it became known as *Monte Carlo Baby*). Because Audrey spoke both languages fluently, Boyer wanted her for both versions. She happily agreed and quickly started packing.

In May, before shooting began, Audrey made four subsequent trips to Paris in preparation for the film. Even though she had been raised in Europe,

OPPOSITE Audrey, photographed by Edward Quinn, in Monte Carlo the summer she met Colette. ABOVE Audrey in East Sussex, England, in May 1951.

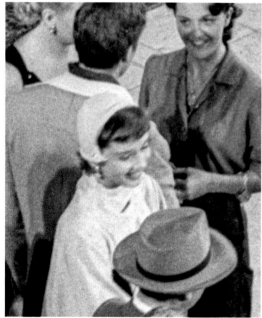

ABOVE Audrey filming *We Will Go to Monte Carlo* in the lobby of the Hôtel de Paris Monte-Carlo.
OPPOSITE Audrey with French actor and dancer Edmond Audran in Monte Carlo.

this was her first time visiting the fashionable city. She was born in Belgium on May 4, 1929, and was the only child of Joseph Hepburn-Ruston, a British banker, and Ella van Heemstra, a Dutch baroness. She spent her infancy in Brussels with her father, mother, and two stepbrothers from her mother's first marriage. "I lived and was based in Belgium until I moved to Holland, so my first words were French," she explained years later.[1]

At the age of five, a year before her father walked out on the family, Audrey was sent to boarding school in England, until the baroness withdrew her and moved the family to the Netherlands in 1939. Audrey studied ballet at the Arnhem School of Music but was forced to suspend her lessons once it was no longer safe to practice due to the German occupation. She spent the duration of World War II in Arnhem until its liberation in 1945. Soon after, Audrey continued her ballet training in Amsterdam with former ballerina Sonia Gaskell, until returning to London with her mother, where she accepted a scholarship at the Marie Rambert School of Ballet. Due to her training, Audrey began booking gigs in musical revues on the West End, effectively earning money from the thing she loved most in the world, dance.

On Saturday, May 26, 1951, Audrey traveled to Paris, unaware of the significance the city would have on her future. She visited the French studio Hoche Productions (founded by Ray Ventura, the producer of *Nous irons à Monte Carlo* and *Monte Carlo Baby*) to finalize her contract and additional wardrobe changes. The following month, prepped and ready to go, Audrey traveled to Monaco to begin production on *We Will Go to Monte Carlo*. While filming in Monte Carlo, Audrey resided at the Hôtel de Paris Monte-Carlo in the heart of Monaco. Established in 1864, the Hôtel de Paris Monte-Carlo was a major attraction for international society. Two of the hotel's most notable residents were the French novelist Sidonie-Gabrielle Colette (known by the monym Colette) and

ABOVE Audrey photographed by Irving Penn for *Vogue*'s
November 1951 issue. OPPOSITE Audrey with Colette at
her Palais-Royal apartment.

her husband, Maurice Goudeket. Colette, who was wheelchair-bound due to severe arthritis, had spent five consecutive winters at the exclusive hotel. Prior to her vacation, Colette had hired playwright Anita Loos and theatrical producer Gilbert Miller to dramatize her novel *Gigi* for the Broadway stage. Everything was in place but one vital part: the actress who would play the starring role of Gigi. Colette knew she needed someone with that certain je ne sais quoi to portray a sixteen-year-old French girl growing up in nineteenth-century Paris.

As legend has it, one afternoon Audrey was shooting a scene in the lobby of the Hôtel de Paris when she caught the eye of Colette, who was passing through on her way to lunch. Amid the frenzy of actors, crew members, and camera equipment,

Colette turned to her husband and exclaimed, "*Voilà notre Gigi pour l'Amérique!*"[2] ("There is my American Gigi!"). At the behest of his wife, Maurice made arrangements to meet Audrey and organize an introduction between Colette and the fledgling young actress. Audrey, admittedly clueless about the author's stature in the literary world, conveyed her doubts. She was terribly flattered by their offer but expressed her regrets, "I'm sorry, madame, but I wouldn't be able to, because I can't act. I'm not equipped to play a leading role since I've never said more than one or two lines on stage in my life. I've done bits in films, of course, but I don't consider that acting."[3]

Defiant in her decision, Colette wouldn't accept anything less than yes. With some convincing,

*Pour Audrey Hepburn,*
*trésor que j'ai trouvé sur*
*une plage !*

*Colette*

Audrey accepted the part of *Gigi* and in July of 1951 traveled to Paris to meet with Colette at her apartment at the Palais-Royal on 9 rue de Beaujolais. Colette's one-bedroom flat was decorated with crimson red carpeting, yellow and gray doors, and a view that overlooked the gardens. She first resided at the Palais-Royal in 1927, eventually leaving in 1929, until she returned nine years later in 1938, settling at her final location on the first floor. Over time Colette became synonymous with the Palais-Royal. Her writing desk was positioned against a window facing out toward the courtyard lined with an allée of linden trees. Here, Colette could let her mind wander. Standing tall behind her was an enclave bookshelf stacked with leather-bound tomes and framed butterfly displays. The day Audrey visited, Colette was dressed in a silk

ABOVE The portrait of Colette inscribed to Audrey.

blouse with polka dots and a lavallière. Her natural curls were wild and her eyes were darkened with black coal.

Colette sensitively wrote about Audrey's arrival, "She is dark and charming, as slender as the swamp reeds of my native province, with an ease and grace of movement such as a doe might envy . . . I saw her for the first time in Monte Carlo, where people turned around to stare after her; and for the second, in the shade of a Paris garden planted by Louis XIII. But I never expected to see her, armed with as much patience as if she were waiting expressly for me, on the old stairway of my Palais-Royal apartment."[4]

Audrey entered the author's dwelling dressed in all black like the beatnik poets who gathered along the Seine. She wore a black long-sleeved sweater with matching slacks, a leather belt that subtly accentuated her delicate waist, and matching black gloves. Her dark hair was cropped and pinned back behind her ears, emphasizing a pair of golden clip-on earrings. She naturally possessed the sophistication of a young Parisian woman. The combination of her boyish appearance and charming disposition made her the perfect embodiment of Colette's precocious heroine. Audrey met with Colette and Gilbert Miller at the author's apartment to discuss the role of Gigi before rehearsals began in New York that September. Miller had coordinated to have a photographer take publicity photos of Colette and her ingenue to commemorate the occasion. The images show Audrey resting her head on Colette's shoulder as Colette read from the book *Fils de Réjane Souvenirs* by Jacques Porel.

During her stay in Paris, Gilbert Miller also arranged for Audrey to have her portrait taken for *Vogue* magazine by American photographer Irving Penn. It was her first time featured in the popular fashion magazine. In 1950, Penn traveled to Paris to shoot his first haute couture collections for *Vogue* at a daylight studio inside an old photography school on the rue de Vaugirard. In the summer of 1951, Penn was once again sent to Paris by *Vogue*, but for a different purpose, to photograph Colette's new discovery. The black-and-white portrait was featured in *Vogue*'s November 1951 issue.

Audrey, who was photographed at the *Vogue* studio in Paris, sat in front of a dark hanging theater carpet and was asked to pose herself for the portrait. She wore the same black ensemble she had worn during her meeting with Colette but this time without the gloves. Her short fringe framed her youthful face. Gently resting her head on the palm of her hand, Audrey looked directly at the camera with a closed smile. Her expression was elfin: sweet and unpretentious with a hint of mischief. The picture's caption read "Audrey Hepburn, star of 'Gigi.'"[5] Little did she know, but Audrey was in store for a whirlwind year. Between rehearsals, publicity, and her impending marriage to James Hanson, the son of a London trucking magnate (they would end their engagement in the fall of 1952), Audrey would fly to Paris three more times for wardrobe fittings before making her Broadway debut that fall.

It would be another two years before Audrey returned to Colette's apartment at the Palais-Royal. In February of 1955, during a three-day trip to Paris, Audrey paid her respects to Maurice Goudeket after the passing of his wife the year before. It was rumored that Colette had left Audrey some valuable jewelry in her will. That August, Audrey traveled to Paris again to attend a mass at a small chapel on the outskirts of Paris, marking the one-year anniversary of Colette's death. Also in attendance were the French actor Maurice Chevalier and the French writer and artist Jean Cocteau. Colette had single-handedly changed the trajectory of Audrey's life; in less than a year, she had gone from being an unknown chorus girl to a brilliant star on the rise. Among her possessions, Audrey faithfully kept a portrait of Colette inscribed "*Pour Audrey Hepburn, trésor que j'ai trouvé sur une plage.*" Translated: "To Audrey Hepburn, a treasure that I found on a beach."[6]

Audrey's sojourn to the Palais-Royal ignited an enduring love affair with Paris. After completing her first stint on Broadway in *Gigi*, Audrey would earn her career-defining role as Princess Ann in Paramount Pictures' *Roman Holiday*. The following year, she would sign on to star as the titular role in Billy Wilder's romantic comedy, *Sabrina*. That summer in 1953, Audrey would once again pack her suitcase and travel to the French capital for another life-altering appointment: this time at 8 rue Alfred de Vigny to meet with a young courtier named Hubert de Givenchy. ✳

# 2

# Sabrina

G*igi* opened in New York at the Fulton Theatre on November 25, 1951. Although critics deemed the plot too "old-fashioned" for modern audiences, there was one component that was undeniable: the inspired newcomer playing the role of Gigi. Newspaper headlines were plastered with Audrey's name. The *New York Times* journalist Brooks Atkinson wrote a glowing review with the headline, "Audrey Hepburn is Captivating." Furthering his praise, he continues, "Miss Hepburn is the one fresh element. As Gigi she develops a full-length character from artless gaucheries in the first act to a stirring emotional climax in the last scene. It is a fine piece of sustained acting that is spontaneous, lucid, and captivating."[7] Before the stage curtains closed, Audrey was already signed with Paramount Pictures to star in William Wyler's next project, *Roman Holiday*, scheduled to film the following year. Audrey's star was on the rise and Hollywood had taken notice. Across the pond, in Paris, another hopeful was experiencing his own meteoric success.

Hubert de Givenchy, born Hubert James Taffin de Givenchy, had dreamed of a life in French couture since his childhood days in Beauvais, France. At the age of seventeen, Hubert abandoned law school and ventured to Paris in pursuit of his boyhood idol, "The King of Fashion," Cristóbal Balenciaga. Unfortunately, Hubert would have to wait until 1953 for the two men to meet, but his resolve to enmesh himself in the world of fashion was not deterred. He studied three years at the École des Beaux-Arts, ultimately leaving to work as an apprentice to French couturier Jacques Fath at his salon on 39 avenue Pierre 1er de Serbie in Paris. Givenchy recalled his time working under the prominent designer: "Jacques Fath, a striking personality, always in a whirl, received me dressed in grey from head to toe, under a wolf coat that hung to the floor. 'You start tomorrow!' With a kind of stupor and provincial terror, I discovered the world of couture. Models and sales women reeking with *Grey Iris* perfume, and giggling punctuated by cries and calls the live-long day, dressing gowns half-open, *mon chéri, mon poulet*, all the while that Jacques Fath tried the model dresses on himself, draping and pinning them on a grosgrain that he held at his waist . . ."[8]

His term with Fath was the start of an incomparable education under the instruction of Robert Piguet, Lucien Lelong, and Elsa Schiaparelli. After his short stint with Fath, Hubert accepted a job with Robert Piguet, a Swiss-born designer who had previously mentored Christian Dior. Hubert stayed for a year before making his way to Lucien Lelong, where he lasted six months. In 1947, Hubert joined Schiaparelli's team as an assistant

OPPOSITE Audrey wearing Givenchy's *Inez de Castro* gown for *Sabrina*.

neo-Gothic mansion, owned by Monsieur Menier, of the French Menier Chocolate Company. The room was a mere fifteen by twenty feet, which he tented off with gray cotton sheets hung high from the wainscoting. With a little encouragement—and financial help—from a backer, he expanded his salon to the second floor, where he would unveil his creations the subsequent month. His team at Givenchy was a small assembly of friends and associates. Philippe Venet, Hubert's companion and loyal friend, left Schiaparelli to join Givenchy as head tailor. Bettina Graziani, one of Paris's top models, joined Givenchy as Hubert's publicist and star mannequin. Last but not least, Janette Mahler, another volunteer from Schiaparelli, was enlisted as his secretary and remained with Hubert until his retirement in 1995. With everything in place, Hubert braced himself as he prepared for the inauguration of Givenchy.

On February 2, 1952, at just twenty-five years old, Hubert de Givenchy debuted his premiere collection. Similar to Audrey's crowd-pleasing performance in *Gigi*, Hubert's designs made an imposing impression on *le tout-Paris*. "The opening of a new house the first day provided the surprise of the season, when twenty-five-year-old, six-foot-three Hubert de Givenchy was given the biggest ovation Paris had seen in five years. His gay, youthful collection, modeled by four of Paris' prettiest mannequins, was shown in the midst of a first-night atmosphere, before a packed and dressy audience which included V.I.P.'s. His modern approach, his intriguing 'separates', his glamorized shirting cottons for evening made a great hit,"[10] wrote Lucette Caron of the *Hartford Courant* magazine. Hubert had seamlessly stationed himself among the haute couture masters such as Christian Dior, Coco Chanel, and his former mentor, Jacques Fath. Fashion experts lauded Hubert; Marie-Louise Bousquet, the editor of Paris *Harper's Bazaar*, even announced Givenchy as the future of French couture.

and creative director of her boutique. He considered his time at Schiaparelli invaluable, stating, "It was here that I came to know true elegance."[9] During his off hours at Schiaparelli, Hubert experimented with the excess fabric left around the workroom. He practiced designing separates by modifying the structure of an average blouse and skirt, resulting in what would later be the crux of his first collection.

Hubert remained with Schiaparelli for four years, eventually resigning to forge his eponymous label, *Givenchy*. In January of 1952, with the financial help of his cousin Hélène Bouilloux-Lafont and his brother-in-law, Louis Fontaine, Hubert opened his first salon on 8 rue Alfred de Vigny overlooking Parc Monceau. His workroom was part of an 1860

ABOVE AND OPPOSITE Hubert de Givenchy at his design house on 8 rue Alfred de Vigny in Paris, 1955.

In another part of the world, on a scorchingly hot summer's day in 1952, Audrey Hepburn was touring the streets of Rome for her first major motion picture, *Roman Holiday*. Her performance as Princess Anne would later earn her the coveted Best Actress award in 1954 at the Academy Awards, the British Academy Film Awards, and the Golden Globes. Audrey was an international success and in 1953 Paramount Pictures wanted her for Billy Wilder's upcoming romantic comedy *Sabrina*, based on the play by Samuel A. Taylor. Wilder's *Sabrina* is the story of a chauffeur's daughter, Sabrina Fairchild (Audrey), who lives with her father over the garage of the Larrabee Estate on Long Island. She spends her days yearning after the boss's son, David Larrabee (William Holden), a directionless yet charismatic playboy. However, her father (John Williams) disapproves of her unrequited crush and enrolls Sabrina in cooking classes in Paris. While abroad, Sabrina finds a renewed spirit in the French capital. She returns home a chic young woman with a new outlook on life, revealing, "I have learned how to live, how to be in the world and of the world, and not just to stand aside and watch. And I will never, never again run away from life, or from love, either." Through a series of events, Sabrina unexpectedly falls for David's older brother, Linus Larrabee (Humphrey Bogart), a reserved man with a penchant for business. In the final scene, Linus abandons his life of responsibility and joins Sabrina on a boat headed toward Paris, to let in *la vie en rose*.

Director Billy Wilder knew from the outset that it was pivotal for his leading lady to wear authentic Parisian designs on her arrival from Paris. Edith Head, a well-established costume designer for Paramount Pictures and a five-time Academy Award winner for Best Costume Design, was contracted to create the costumes for *Sabrina*.

Head had previously worked with Audrey on *Roman Holiday* and was enchanted by Audrey's European aristocratic appearance. "[Audrey's] figure and flair told me, at once, here was a girl who'd been born to make designers happy. If she were not an actress she'd be a model or a designer. As it is, she's all three: a girl way ahead of high fashion, who deliberately looks different from other women, who has dramatized her own slenderness into her chief asset,"[11] Head shared in her 1959 autobiography *The Dress Doctor*.

However, Audrey Wilder, Billy Wilder's wife, wanted to explore a different avenue; she proposed the idea of hiring a true French couturier to design the costumes instead. Imaginably, Edith Head was vexed by the decision: "The director broke my heart by suggesting that, while the chauffeur's daughter was in Paris, she actually buy a Paris suit."[12] Gladys de Segonzac, wife of the managing director of Paramount's Paris office, Edouard de Segonzac, contacted Balenciaga, who regrettably turned down their offer. He was in the midst of preparing his Autumn collection (which would be shown in late July) and could not provide designs under the time restraints. Without a moment to spare, Gladys picked up the phone and called Paris's new boy wonder, Hubert de Givenchy.

Filming for *Sabrina* had been delayed until September of 1953, providing Audrey the opportunity to take a vacation with her mother through continental Europe. The studio executives concocted a plan for Audrey to visit Paris during her holiday and purchase the key pieces for Sabrina's Parisian wardrobe. Under the guise that Audrey was purchasing these items for her personal closet, Paramount could bypass custom fees and avoid crediting Givenchy for his designs, a stipulation they kept from Audrey. She was to visit Givenchy's salon on 8 rue Alfred de Vigny to select one dark suit ("This should be of the type she would wear crossing the Atlantic by plane and

arrive upstate New York by train"), several blouses to be worn with the suit, two "extreme French hats appropriate for the suit," and one "very smart French day dress," according to the production notes written by producer Frank Caffey.[13]

Audrey arrived in Paris that July and was greeted by a very confused staff at Givenchy. Hubert and his team were anticipating the arrival of a different Ms. Hepburn. When Gladys had reached out earlier, they assumed she meant Katharine Hepburn, the legendary stage and screen actress. They were befuddled by the appearance of the delicate stranger standing before them. Hubert remembers his first impression of Audrey on that fateful day: "[She wore]

OPPOSITE Audrey wearing her Oxford gray suit at the Glen Cove train station during the production of *Sabrina*, 1953. ABOVE Audrey with director Billy Wilder on the set of *Sabrina*.

a very strange ensemble. She had on very slim pants, capri pants, with ballerina shoes, a little white T-shirt and a gondolier hat—imagine this is in Paris!—with a red ribbon across the top. And no makeup. She looked like a ballet dancer."[14] Like Balenciaga, Hubert was hard at work preparing for his Autumn collection. "I told Audrey that I had very few workers and I needed all hands to help me with my next collection, which I had to show very soon. But she insisted, 'Please, please, there must be something I can try on.'"[15] He directed her toward the remaining samples from his 1953 Spring Summer collection. Audrey's face lit up as she carefully ran her fingers over the beautiful textiles proudly displayed before her. Of the pieces, she selected an Oxford gray double-breasted wool ottoman suit with a scoop neck and slim skirt. "The way she moved in the suit, she was so happy. She said that it was exactly what she wanted for the movie. She gave a life to the clothes—she had a way of installing herself in them that I have seen in no one else since, except maybe the model Dalma. The suit just adapted to her. Something magic happened. Suddenly she felt good—you could feel her excitement, her joy,"[16] Hubert described to *Vanity Fair* journalist Amy Fine Collins in 1995. Audrey paired the suit with a snug turban made of pleated white satin, which she wore in the film when Sabrina arrived at the Glen Cove Rail Station in Long Island.

The next item Audrey tried on was a strapless evening gown known as the "Inez De Castro." "I have a lovely evening dress with yards of skirt and way off the shoulder. Shall I wear it?" Sabrina exclaims when she accepts an invitation to the annual Larrabee party. The gown was constructed of white organdy and embroidered with an eighteenth-century floral motif made of black silk yarn and threaded with black beads and clusters of white French knot embroidery. The sheath underskirt was worn under a detachable flared overskirt edged with black organdy ruffles. Hubert originally presented the gown with a jacket of black jersey worn over the bodice; that item was not used in the film, but Audrey kept the garment for her personal wardrobe and was later photographed wearing the jacket at the Ice Follies Show in 1954.

Hubert and his staff were breathless at the sight of Audrey. Moments ago she had been a nameless girl from off the street, but now standing before them was an elegant young woman with perfect posture, a piquant face, and a short coiffed haircut that emphasized her beautifully pronounced jawline. Wearing the Inez de Castro, she was Givenchy's ideal mannequin. Dreda Mele, the *directrice* of Givenchy, who had also worn the Inez de Castro gown to a ball, remembers that day candidly: "[Audrey] was like the arrival of a summer flower. She was *lumineuse*—radiant, in both a physical and spiritual sense. I felt immediately how lovely she was, inside and out. Though she came to Givenchy out of the blue, there is no doubt that they were made to meet. Audrey was always very definite in her taste and look. She came to him because she was attracted by the image he could give her. And she entered that image totally. She entered into his dream, too. I repeat, they were made for each other."[17]

The last dress Audrey chose was a black satin cocktail dress finished from a ribbed cotton pique produced by the fabric house Abraham. Audrey had the original design modified to fit her specific needs for *Sabrina*. The final version worn in the film had a boat neckline with small bows fastened at the shoulders. The back of the bodice was cut into a daring V shape with buttons clasped down the backside and a cinched waist that accentuated the volume of the full ballerina-length skirt. Audrey tried on an assortment of hats available in the

OPPOSITE Audrey, wearing her black satin cocktail dress, with Humphrey Bogart on the set of *Sabrina*.

workroom, choosing a medieval-style chapeau of black satin embellished with rhinestones. Despite her undisputed beauty, Audrey was plagued by her own insecurities. She often criticized the size of her feet, the length of her neck, her crooked teeth, and what she considered her skinny collarbones. Hubert altered the neckline of the dress to hide her

ABOVE Audrey with Hubert during a dress fitting in Rome, 1958.

collarbones and emphasize her attractive shoulders. "What used to be called a *décolleté bateau*," Givenchy said. "Afterwards it was called the *décolleté* Sabrina."[18]

The staff at Givenchy were amazed by Audrey's unique sense of fashion. "Audrey always added a twist, something piquant, amusing, to the clothes," Hubert commented. "Though of course I advised her, she knew precisely what she wanted. She knew herself very well—for example, which is her good profile and which is her bad. She was very professional. No detail ever escaped her. Billy Wilder approved of everything she chose, and so I gave them the samples to use for the movie. Billy's only concern was that the clothes adapt to the form of her face. They had to all correspond to the *visage*."[19]

Hubert allowed Audrey to use the pieces she had selected and invited her to dine at a bistro on the rue de Grenelle. There was a spiritual connection between the two: "Before the dinner was over I told her, 'I'll do anything for you,'"[20] Hubert proclaimed. Audrey and Hubert both came from aristocratic families and demonstrated a profound appreciation for the arts at an early age. They bonded over losing their fathers when they were young—Hubert's father had passed away when he was two and Audrey's had abandoned the family when she was six. They shared a love of gardens, the countryside, clothes, and the color white. "Wherever they went, everything was white. I always thought that was—not strange, but indicative of her: Everything had to be white," actress Deborah Kerr revealed.[21] Audrey and Hubert's relationship was a lifelong friendship that would generate an indelible impact on fashion and film.

Audrey returned to Hollywood with her newest purchases in hand. Billy Wilder and the production team were satisfied with her selections for Sabrina's metamorphosis. From September through November, Audrey bounced between coasts, filming in both New York and Los Angeles. Months later, Audrey invited Hubert to California to attend a private screening of *Sabrina*. As the credits rolled, an egregious transgression appeared before their eyes. Next to the words "Costume Supervision" was the name Edith Head. Audrey was horrified by the omission of Hubert de Givenchy's name. Hubert was equally surprised. Edith Head was a proud woman who ran Paramount's costume department with an iron fist. It was an open secret in Hollywood that Head couldn't draw. She hired a team of skilled sketch artists to produce drawings for her approval before adding her signature. Head had been chief designer at Paramount since 1938 and had it written into her contract that she was to receive credit as sole designer. According to the book *Audrey Style*, Billy Wilder didn't choose Head for *Sabrina*, but rather she herself had chosen to work on the film, since she had been given top priority for all first-class pictures at Paramount. Audrey Wilder would later confide in author Pamela Keogh that Edith Head received credit for *Sabrina* because Hubert didn't qualify for the Costumers Union. On March 30, 1955, Edith Head won the Oscar for Best Costume Design for *Sabrina*. She declined to give an acceptance speech.

"Imagine if I had received credit for *Sabrina* then, at the beginning of my career. It would have helped," Hubert recounted. "But it doesn't matter—a few years passed, and then everyone knew. Anyway, what could I do? I didn't really care. I was so pleased to dress Miss Hepburn."[22] Despite their disappointment, their budding friendship only grew stronger. Audrey and Hubert worked together until Audrey's death in 1993. They would collaborate on eight more films, including their next picture, the 1957 movie musical *Funny Face*. Hubert would continue to dress Audrey on-screen and in her private life. He designed her gowns for premieres, award shows, and intimate family occasions, like the silk dress Audrey wore to her son Sean's christening in 1960 and the pink wool minidress she sported at her wedding in 1969. "For me," Hubert recounted in the book *The Givenchy Style*, "she was a gift from on high. Thanks to her grace and kindness, we always found it a great pleasure to be in one another's company. It was as if there were a hidden conspiracy between us."[23] ✳

# { 3 }
# Three Days in Paris

Nineteen fifty-four would prove to be a triumphant year for the budding starlet. Within the same month, Audrey would earn two of the highest acting awards in the United States. On March 25, she took home the Best Actress Oscar for her performance in *Roman Holiday*, and three days later she won the Tony for Best Lead Actress in a Play for *Ondine*. Audrey was enjoying the accolades of her fortuitous year, but after an arduous stint on Broadway, Audrey and her *Ondine* costar, Mel Ferrer (who was twelve years her senior), retreated to the restorative mountainside of Bürgenstock, Switzerland. On September 25, after a short courtship, Audrey and Mel were married during a small private ceremony at a Protestant chapel surrounded by their closest friends and family. Following their quick honeymoon in Rome, Audrey resumed work and began her international promotional tour for *Sabrina*. On February 21, 1955, the newlyweds arrived in Paris for a marathon three days involving press, a private viewing of *Sabrina*, and a Givenchy fashion show.

This visit to Paris was unlike Audrey's previous excursions. She was now a full-fledged movie star and her influence was seen everywhere in the French capital. Young Parisian girls were sporting her urchin haircut from *Roman Holiday* and fashion mannequins emulated Audrey's modern style. She was no longer the unknown starlet whom Hubert had mistaken for Katharine Hepburn. Her popularity had reached new heights and was rapidly approaching the pinnacle of fame.

Audrey's three-day trip was arranged by Paramount for the premiere of *Sabrina*. On their arrival in Paris that Monday afternoon, the Ferrers were immediately rushed from the Orly airport to the Ritz Hotel, where ten hotel employees were ordered to patrol the entry to room 24. It appeared that the Parisian press was not happy about the tight security shielding the newlyweds. The two actors rushed from their rented Cadillac straight into the lobby of the Ritz, choosing to avoid photos and interviews. After settling in, their first stop was cocktails with John B. Nathan, the manager of Paramount International films division for Europe, at his home on avenue Foch. Promptly following drinks at Nathan's apartment, Audrey and Mel made their way to La Crémaillère restaurant located on Place Beauvau. En route, cameramen desperately pursued the elusive couple by car, while Audrey did her best to shield her face against the flashing camera bulbs. The Ferrers arrived at the restaurant shortly after 9:00 P.M. and were accompanied by American humorist Art Buchwald. The three friends enjoyed a private meal without interruption. Audrey had a bowl of consommé, a slice of salmon, and a dish of praline ice cream.

OPPOSITE Audrey photographed in her suite at the Ritz Paris.

ABOVE TOP Audrey and Mel Ferrer signing autographs on their arrival in Paris. ABOVE BOTTOM Audrey and Mel outside the Ritz Paris. OPPOSITE Audrey at the *Sabrina* press conference.

The next day, Audrey met with Paramount representatives for a business lunch before arriving at a private screening of *Sabrina* dubbed entirely in French. This was Audrey's second time viewing *Sabrina* in Paris. Earlier that month, on February 4, she had attended the official French premiere of *Sabrina* at the American Embassy at the Hôtel de Talleyrand located on rue Saint-Florentin. Audrey had been every bit as elegant as her on-screen persona. Dressed in Sabrina's black-and-white Givenchy ball gown, the Inez de Castro, Audrey had looked as though she had glided off the screen and onto the carpet. There had been many well-known actors in attendance, including Marlene Dietrich, who wore a Dior burgundy silk taffeta evening ensemble, and the renowned entertainer Josephine Baker. As Audrey had made her way through the halls of the American Embassy she was taken aback at the sight of Ms. Baker. Despite her recent success, Audrey was still that young chorus girl at heart and was no doubt starstruck. After the premiere, Audrey had attended a dinner hosted by the French magazine *Jours de France* at La Tour d'Argent.

On the night of February 22, at 6:00 P.M., after leaving the private screening of *Sabrina*, Audrey joined reporters at the Ritz Hotel for a press conference and cocktails. It was the first time journalists had been allowed to interview the young actress since her arrival the day before. The Parisian press were frustrated by the limited access they were given to the in-demand actress. However, Audrey dazzled the journalists in a classic black cocktail dress worn with a pair of pearl earrings and minimal makeup that emphasized her famous doe eyes. Audrey's cocktail dress was a well-coordinated publicity stunt orchestrated by Hubert de Givenchy and *Harper's Bazaar* editor in chief, Carmel Snow. This particular design was an American copy of one of Givenchy's French models, created for the American market. The black, slim-fit dress had a simplicity in its design unique to Givenchy. The

dress's most notable detail was the straight neck-line with *collar à revers* that complemented the dress's narrow cut.

Mel remained in their hotel room while Audrey, speaking in perfect French, graciously answered questions and denied the never-ending pregnancy rumors. "No, really. I'm not expecting a baby," she assured the journalist, immediately adding, "I hope I will be able to have children in the future."[24] Unbeknownst to everyone in the room, Audrey was keeping a secret. She was indeed pregnant but would sadly suffer a miscarriage in March. Regardless of the intrusive questions, Audrey happily smiled for pictures. She posed in front of a fireplace, next to a bust of Marie Antoinette, and in front of a large tap-estry before she retreated behind a pink azalea plant for cover. The press inquired about future projects, including the newest Otto Preminger movie, *Bonjour*

*Tristesse*, based on the book by Françoise Sagan, and a movie adaptation of *L'Aiglon*, a play by Edmond Rostand. Audrey disclosed that the rights to *L'Aiglon* had been purchased and that two English writers had begun work on the screenplay. There was also talk about her *Roman Holiday* director, William Wyler, directing the movie the following year in Vienna. But the role Audrey was most interested in playing was that of Viola from *Twelfth Night*. Lastly, she was questioned about a possible film version of *Ondine*. Audrey and Mel were all set to reprise their roles as Ondine and Hans on the silver screen, but, for now, all four projects had yet to be confirmed by Audrey or the studios. (Unfortunately, *Ondine*, *L'Aiglon*, and *Twelfth Night* would never see the light of day.)

Although her husband skipped the conference, Audrey was not alone; she was joined by her *Gigi* director, Raymond Rouleau, and the famous French bandleader Ray Ventura. Audrey was delighted to see her former friends and colleagues. Ray was one of the producers and actors in *We Will Go to Monte Carlo*, the movie where Audrey had first met Colette. Also in attendance was the young actress Evelyne Ker, who was currently starring in the French production of *Gigi*. Dressed casually in a red sweater, Evelyne rushed over to Audrey and excitedly kissed her on the cheek. After the press conference concluded, Audrey, Mel, and Ray made their way to Le Berkeley restaurant where the three ate crêpes suzette. Audrey confided in Ray that she had every intention of turning down the lead in *Bonjour Tristesse* despite the press's encouragement, because she felt the character wasn't sympathetic. Later that year in August, Audrey sat down with Françoise Sagan, the author of *Bonjour Tristesse*, during an afternoon tea at the Hôtel Ritz. Feeling a tinge of regret, Audrey amiably declined the lead role of Cécile. She was already committed to Billy Wilder's next project, *Love in the Afternoon*. The part of Cécile eventually went to a promising young American actress, Jean Seberg.

On February 23, her last day in Paris, Audrey's schedule was filled with back-to-back engagements. Her first appointment was lunch at the Dutch Embassy before meeting with Hubert de Givenchy at his atelier on rue Alfred de Vigny. Audrey and Mel sat together as they eagerly observed Givenchy's fashion show for his Spring collection. Once again, the press was not permitted entrance. The *Sydney Morning Herald* noted, "Thwarted Parisian journalist are prophesying that Miss Hepburn will ask to be surrounded by an artificial fog during her fittings."[25]

Givenchy dedicated his newest collection to his young muse. His latest pieces showcased simple, elongated silhouettes and introduced new colors like soft yellows, dark pinks, and porcelain blues. Bettina Graziani, Hubert's go-to mannequin and former press agent, flew in from Ireland

OPPOSITE Audrey, Raymond Rauleau, and Evelyne Ker at the *Sabrina* press conference held at the Ritz Paris. ABOVE TOP Audrey and Mel dining in Paris. ABOVE BOTTOM Audrey with Maurice Goudeket at Colette's apartment at the Palais-Royal.

just for the occasion. Graziani opened the fashion show wearing the famous "Bettina" blouse, a white poplin blouse with black eyelet scalloped sleeves named for his favorite model, which Audrey ordered in both black and white. Audrey purchased several dresses from Givenchy's collection, including a white strapless dress in organdy embroidered with silk threads in a subtle floral motif and a grosgrain sleeveless afternoon dress in light pink with soft white lines. (In June, while in Rome, Audrey was photographed by Norman Parkinson wearing the pink grosgrain dress for *Glamour* magazine's December 1955 issue.)

At the fashion show, Audrey came face-to-face with Jacky Mazel, one of Givenchy's models who was often described as Audrey's doppelgänger. Tall and slim, with a similar complexion and bone structure, the two Givenchy darlings bore a striking resemblance that would often confuse the public. Even the *Daily Mail* newspaper mistakenly captioned a photo of Jacky as Audrey.

Since Audrey had little time for shopping she asked her dear friend (and Givenchy model) Capucine to order a few items on her behalf. Audrey ordered a set of luggage at Louis Vuitton, including a makeup case, a small briefcase, and a medium-sized suitcase. She purchased a few pairs of shoes by André Perugia, Givenchy's shoemaker, and cotton pants and knitwear from Rodier boutique. At Cartier, Mel bought Audrey a gold-plated minaudière (a decorative compact handbag) as a small gift to remember their trip.

That evening, the married couple invited Raymond Rouleau to their hotel room for cocktails. The Ferrers had plans to visit Maurice Goudeket, Colette's widow, at his late wife's apartment at the Palais-Royal. Audrey and Mel carefully constructed a plan to divert the attention of the persistent photographers waiting in the lobby. At approximately seven thirty that evening, Raymond left the room to inform the cameramen that Audrey and Mel had retired to their hotel suite and wouldn't be making any further appearances that evening. As instructed by the Ferrers, their chauffeur pulled the Cadillac around to the back entrance of the Ritz, where Audrey and Mel ran from the side service entrance directly into the car.

At Colette's apartment, one photographer, Jack Garofalo, a friend of Maurice, was granted permission to photograph the two actors as they reminisced with their old friend. The images were published in March in *Paris Match* magazine. Colette's apartment at the Palais-Royal had remained unchanged since Audrey's first visit back in 1951. Portraits of Colette still hung on the walls in remembrance of the beloved author.

Audrey's feverish seventy-two hours finally came to an end. Despite the Parisians' disappointment by the actress's disappearing act and lack of press, there was no ill will between the two. Audrey had enjoyed her brief tour of Paris, and she left the city with a number of new Givenchy dresses and the promise of returning soon. Then the couple was off yet again. Audrey and Mel would return home to their small chalet in Switzerland for a moment of respite before traveling to Rome for their newest project, *War and Peace*, where the real-life couple played the romantic leads. Audrey would return to Paris in the winter of 1956 for wardrobe fittings at Givenchy's atelier for her next project, *Funny Face*. ✳

OPPOSITE Audrey and Mel watch as model Jacky Mazel walks the Givenchy fashion show.

# Funny Face

With three movies under her belt, Audrey was now the highest-paid actress in Hollywood. The success of her last two films secured her an enormous upgrade, toppling her female contemporaries such as Elizabeth Taylor and Grace Kelly. Audrey negotiated a staggering $350,000 deal for the role of Natasha Rostova in *War and Peace*. It was hard to believe that in 1953 she had earned a mere $15,000 for her previous picture, *Sabrina*.

In the spring of 1955, Audrey and Mel rented a villa in the Alban Hills, just twenty miles outside Rome, where they would remain throughout the filming of *War and Peace*. After completing an intensive shoot, Audrey and Mel relocated to their long-term rental property, a small chalet in Bürgenstock, Switzerland, before packing their suitcases and heading off to Paris for preproduction preparations for *Funny Face*.

*Funny Face* was Audrey's first movie musical. The original 1927 Broadway stage musical had been composed by Ira and George Gershwin and starred Audrey's *Funny Face* costar, Fred Astaire, and his sister, Adele. The new and improved Hollywood version heavily deviated from the 1927 stage version. *Funny Face* the movie was a modernized Cinderella story about an intellectual named Jo

Stockton (Audrey) whose world is turned upside down when Dick Avery (Fred Astaire), a fashion photographer for *Quality* magazine, notices untapped modeling potential in the modest bookstore clerk from Greenwich Village. Jo is flown from New York to Paris to present the newest fashion collection by French couturier Paul Duval, whose character was inspired by Hubert de Givenchy. Two of the main characters, Dick Avery and Maggie Prescott (Kay Thompson), were loosely based on the real lives of American fashion photographer Richard Avedon and *Harper's Bazaar* fashion editor Diana Vreeland.

*Funny Face* is a colorful sensation directed by Stanley Donen, who masterfully bonds the worlds of Gershwin and fashion with innovative camera techniques centered in the chic backdrop of Paris. Jo's trajectory isn't too dissimilar from Audrey's own success story. Both women were unknowns discovered by prominent industry players who catapulted their careers practically overnight. *Funny Face* didn't make a splash at the box office, but critics agreed that Audrey was perfectly cast as the gamine model. Her soft vocals and energized dance numbers captivated audiences. With the help of Hubert de Givenchy's mouthwatering confections, *Funny Face* earned the status of fashion cult favorite.

Before production began in the spring of 1956, Audrey spent two months in Paris studying with Lucien Legrand, the first dancer and choreographer

OPPOSITE Audrey with makeup artist Frank McCoy on the set of *Funny Face*.

of the Paris Opera Ballet. Audrey had studied ballet as a child and danced in stage musicals in London after World War II, but this was her first time performing in a movie musical. It had been years since Audrey had attended dance classes; she was out of practice and insecure about her technique. As she explained to journalist Bob Thomas, "I've been in training for it, and it's quite difficult getting back into shape. I haven't danced professionally for four years, and I haven't even had the time to keep up my lessons."[26]

Under the direction of Legrand, Audrey trained in a small studio at the Paris Ballet. She worked tirelessly with Legrand, whom she respectfully addressed as "Monsieur." Paris was experiencing one of its coldest winters and the studio where they practiced reached freezing temperatures.

Despite the unpleasant conditions, Audrey continued to show up daily wearing her staple uniform consisting of a black wool blouse and black wool tights, both for warmth, and a pair of size 8AA ballet slippers. She was a serious student, often the first one to arrive and the last one to leave. Audrey's strict nature was directly linked to her former ballet instructors Sonia Gaskell and Marie Rambert. "Ballet taught me discipline," she shared with journalist Mark Nichols, who was there to observe one of Audrey's lessons. "Ballet teaches you to make every movement and gesture meaningful."[27] Eugene Loring, the movie's choreographer, marveled at her commitment, remarking, "She endows every movement with quality and lyrical expression."[28] Fred Astaire, who worked with the greats such as Cyd Charisse and Ginger Rogers, agreed with Loring's praise: "Audrey's extremely talented, and learns with amazing speed."[29] However, Audrey felt differently. No matter how many hours she devoted to practicing she still felt unsure of herself. "I'll never be better than adequate," she professed to Nichols.[30] Her long absence from dancing plagued her with self-doubt, but her diligence paid off in the end.

ABOVE AND OPPOSITE Audrey at a dance class with Lucien Legrand at the Paris Ballet.

Audrey's time was divided between ballet classes and wardrobe fittings at Givenchy's studio on 8 rue Alfred de Vigny. Once again, Paramount Pictures appointed Edith Head as head costume designer, but as with *Sabrina*, Hubert de Givenchy was selected to design Audrey's Parisian wardrobe. Edith wasn't pleased by her downgraded status but, being a seasoned professional, she knew better than to object. She was in charge of Audrey's New York beatnik attire, including her black wool slacks, cashmere sweater, leather moccasins, and

fleece-lined beige raincoat (all of which Audrey requested to keep after filming). Audrey and Hubert began discussing Jo's wardrobe in December. This was Audrey's second time wearing his clothes on the silver screen. In 1953, Audrey had visited Hubert at his atelier for the movie *Sabrina* and under the direction of Paramount Pictures, she had hand selected pieces for Sabrina's fashion evolution. But this was Audrey's first time participating in the preliminary stages of the collaborative process. The two friends relished the opportunity.

Hubert knew he had a demanding job ahead of him. Jo's Parisian wardrobe required ensembles suitable for the Paris runway, and it was essential that Hubert adhere to the color requirements requested by the movie's cinematographer, Ray June. Hubert

ABOVE Audrey with Hubert de Givenchy during a *Funny Face* dress fitting at his atelier. OPPOSITE Audrey inside the Louvre wearing Givenchy's red gown and the Duchess of Windsor's necklace.

designed a total of thirteen costumes, which were part of his 1956 Spring collection. Audrey's Parisian wardrobe cost the studio over $13,000, a significant amount that was comparable to the value of a house in 1956. But Givenchy's designs were worth every penny and the fashion duo proved to be a harmonious pairing. Hubert's timeless pieces transformed Audrey and filled her with confidence. "I'm always inspired by Miss Hepburn when I look for my own mannequins," Hubert told *Photoplay* magazine. "She has the ideal face and figure, with her long, slim body and swan-like neck. It's a real pleasure to make clothes for her."[31]

Although Audrey, Fred, Kay, and even Paris were considered the main stars of *Funny Face*, Hubert's designs made an impact that forever influenced the world of fashion. One of Hubert's ensembles that took center stage was an emerald-green taffeta cape, made by fabric from the textile house Coudurier-Fructus-Descher, worn over a strapless white dress with a two-tiered skirt made of Chantilly lace made by the manufacturer Marescot. Audrey wore the jewel-toned showstopper as she marched down the stairs of the Opéra Garnier. "You're walking out of the opera, leaving to the lush, passionate music of *Tristan und Isolde*. You're very unhappy." Dick illustrates to Jo. "What happened now?" she asks. "A rendezvous at the opera. Two seats. He didn't show up. You're furious. When I say go, walk down with fire in your eyes and murder on your mind." Embodying the grace of a ballerina, Audrey struts down the steps of the opera house, indignantly flipping her cape to reveal the lace skirt hidden underneath. The ensemble was part of Givenchy's haute couture collection and cost a hefty $1,515.

In a romantic sequence between Jo and Dick, in the pastoral countryside outside Paris, Audrey wears a ballerina-length wedding gown designed by Hubert specifically for the movie. The dress consists of a white satin bodice and full skirt made of silk point d'esprit. The length of the silhouette is cut short to allow movement for Audrey as she dances with Astaire across the green landscape. The wedding dress is paired with a white silk point d'esprit hooded veil and adorned with a delicate bow fashioned at the center. The wedding dress cost the studio $1,000. Donen requested that Hubert design two identical white wedding gowns, one that would be waiting for Audrey on her arrival in Paris and a duplicate she would deliver with her from Hollywood.

In a climactic scene in the film, Jo's transformation from bookworm to high fashion model is heralded by Duval's proud announcement to the room of wary critics: "Friends, you saw enter here a waif, a gamin, a lowly caterpillar. We open the cocoon but it is not a butterfly that emerges. No, it is a bird of paradise. Lights! Curtain!" An instrumental version of Gershwin's "'S Wonderful" begins to play. The stage curtains guarding the runway lift in a dramatic effect and standing before them is indeed a *bird of paradise*. The camera slowly pans toward Audrey, who is posed like a marble statue, draped in a creamy shade of pink and stark white. Her hair is slicked back, embellished only by a diamond necklace worn as a tiara. She is wearing a strapless floor-length gown made of white silk with a silk band along the neckline and a back panel that falls separate from the skirt. The train of the pink bodice trails behind her as she glides down the runway. The spectacular creation from Givenchy's haute couture collection is a triumph and leaves the audience yearning for more.

The same silhouette is shown again during a scene filmed at the Louvre. Audrey, in front of the *Winged Victory of Samothrace*, descends a staircase wearing a striking red floor-length gown with matching chiffon stole. Hanging from her swan-like neck, a jeweled necklace worth thousands of dollars belonging to the Duchess of Windsor. The necklace, which had been gifted to the duchess the year before by her husband the duke, consisted of diamonds and Colombian emeralds. Diana Vreeland, fashion editor at *Harper's Bazaar*, had accompanied Audrey to her final fitting for the red gown at Givenchy's atelier. It was there that Diana had the ingenious idea of pairing the red ensemble with the extravagant piece of jewelry. She had seen the duchess showing off the necklace at a recent dinner and approached her about creating a replica for *Funny Face*. In good faith, the duchess actually loaned Audrey the original for a single day. The necklace took center stage as Audrey pranced through the Louvre with the brilliant gems pressed against her chest. At the bottom of the staircase, with his camera in hand, Dick Avery waits for the imminent reveal. "Holy Moses! You look fabulous!" Dick exclaims at the sight of Jo. Jo begins to float down the staircase when Dick screams, "Stop!" Jo smiles and cries, "I don't want to stop. I like it. Take the picture! Take the picture!" Snap! The screen freezes. Stanley Donen works his bit of movie magic. An image of Audrey cloaked in scarlet against a stone background holds for several seconds. She is bewitching.

The clothes were designed in Paris at Givenchy's atelier and entrusted for safekeeping to the managing director of Paramount's Paris office, Edouard de Segonzac. Gladys de Segonzac, Edouard's wife and the wardrobe supervisor on *Funny Face*, was the woman responsible for introducing Audrey to

OPPOSITE Audrey filming a scene for *Funny Face* at the Opéra Garnier.

ABOVE TOP Audrey and Fred Astaire at the Tuileries Gardens. ABOVE MIDDLE Audrey in front of the Paris skyline. ABOVE BOTTOM Kay Thompson, Audrey, and Fred Astaire at a cocktail party given at the Hôtel Raphaël. OPPOSITE Audrey with the *Funny Face* crew on a rainy day at the Tuileries Gardens.

Hubert. She had previously worked with Audrey in *Sabrina* and adored the delicate actress, declaring: "Audrey can wear anything, with taste and dignity. And her patience in fittings is extraordinary. She can stand for hours at a time, never fidgets, never squirms. You know how tired she must be, but she never mentions it. She makes her changes with amazing rapidity, with never a wasted motion."[32] Audrey's *Funny Face* costumes were considered an achievement by both critics and fans and secured Audrey as one of fashion's burgeoning cover girls.

*Funny Face* officially began production on April 9, 1956, at Paramount studios in Hollywood, California. Audrey and Mel rented director Anatole Litvak's home in Malibu. As per her contract, the studio sent a car every day to pick up Audrey and drive her to and from set. In the months following, they filmed the interior scenes before packing up and flying back to Paris to complete the exterior shots. Audrey and Mel arrived in Paris in early June for the final month of production. They made arrangements to stay at their home away from home, the Hôtel Raphaël. The Ferrers were regulars at the Hôtel Raphaël and on a first-name basis with the staff. They invariably booked the same suite each visit, room 312. Mel was in Paris filming his latest movie, *Elena and Her Men* (*Elena et les Hommes*), starring Ingrid Bergman. Although the couple were both based in Paris, their busy itineraries kept them apart. On June 7, Jean Prouvost, the owner of *Paris Match* magazine, hosted a cocktail party at the Hôtel Raphaël in honor of the film's three stars. Members of the press from important foreign publications were in attendance and enjoying the endless glasses of Cinzano on ice. Also present was the very popular French actress Michèle Morgan, who would begin production on *The Vintage* with Mel that August.

Paris had just experienced one of its coldest winters on record and it was followed by a very wet spring. Newspaper headlines announced

it as the "Coldest June since 1886."[33] From the moment the cast and crew arrived, a downpour of rain drenched the city. The unexpected showers complicated Donen's filming schedule and set the studio behind by two weeks and about $300,000. They had to make quick adjustments to the script to incorporate the unanticipated weather. Donen found creative ways to work around the temperamental rains. It had been pouring all day when they first filmed the background shots at the Tuileries Gardens, but when they returned a couple of days later to shoot close-ups, the rain had suddenly stopped. To achieve continuity, the crew simulated the rain by dousing the ground with a water hose. Sadly, their situation did not improve over the course of filming and there wasn't much that could be done. Donen made do and bought three dozen umbrellas for his entire team.

Despite the challenging weather, Donen and his crew were still able to cover a lot of territory. They shot at nearly thirty-five locations including the Eiffel Tower, the Opéra Garnier, the Louvre, Notre Dame, the Arc de Triomphe, Sacre-Coeur, Latona Fountain, the Champs-Elysées, and the Seine River.

Undeterred by the unfavorable circumstances, Audrey remained optimistic. "How lucky can you be for your first musical? First to have a great star like Fred Astaire as your leading man. Then to film most of it in Paris, a city which I adore above all others. We have been filming inside the famous Paris Opera and the Louvre, usually between midnight and six o'clock in the morning when they are closed to the public, with film projectors blazing all over the place.

ABOVE Audrey and Fred Astaire filming their dance number in Chantilly, France.

It's tiring, but with a man of Fred Astaire's energy I am not tired for long. He is such fun to work with. I have just to look at him and I want to laugh. As a title *Funny Face* is an inspiration."[34]

The unpredictable weather combined with the congested city streets called for immediate action. The cast and crew adjusted their itinerary and began filming before dawn and late into the night. One of the more difficult shoots to complete was the final scene of the movie. Audrey, wearing her custom Givenchy wedding dress, dances with Fred Astaire in front of an idyllic chapel on the outskirts of Paris. After weeks of searching for the perfect chapel, the crew discovered Château de la Reine Blanche, a nineteenth-century hunting lodge in Chantilly, France, about twenty miles outside Paris. The crew modified the building by changing the doors and windows to create a picturesque background for two musical numbers including the finale. The scenes required Audrey and Fred to perform "'S Wonderful" and "He Loves and She Loves" on the lawn outside the lodge.

Due to the freezing winter and torrential spring, the grass outside their makeshift chapel was in dire conditions. It was impossible for Audrey and Fred to walk on the thick bog, let alone dance. The sludge ruined several pairs of Audrey's expensive white satin heels, which had been designed by René Mancini. Tensions were high and Audrey could see the frustration in everyone's faces. She knew how to lighten the mood. With a little levity in her eyes, Audrey quipped, "Here I've been waiting twenty years to dance with Fred Astaire, and what do I get? Mud in my eye!"[35]

It was producer Roger Edens who ultimately saved the day. Roger ordered several truckloads of sod from a nearby racetrack to cover the damaged turf. Thankfully, the sod was the perfect solution. At long last, the weary duo were able to complete their final number and return home after a long day.

Performing with Fred was a dream come true for the former dancer, who exclaimed, "Dancing with Fred Astaire! I was so nervous at first I didn't think I could ever do it. Suddenly, you're face to face with someone you have grown up watching in the movies! It was almost too much for me."[36] Before falling into acting, Audrey had aspired to become a professional ballerina. Never in her wildest fantasies could she have imagined frolicking on-screen with the legendary Fred Astaire.

Audrey and Fred were first introduced during a rehearsal session for *Funny Face* at a Hollywood studio prior to filming. Audrey recalls being in a state of nerves the first time they met: "I remember being so shaken that I threw up my breakfast. Stanley, himself having been a dancer, was remarkably encouraging, but on that particular day I was ready to crumble that no words of comfort from anyone could have sufficed."[37] Audrey had lost years of ballet training during World War II, and her two months of instruction under the direction of Lucien Legrand wasn't enough time to rebuild her confidence: "I was terribly apprehensive. I do remember the first time I met Fred Astaire and that was on set. Can you imagine? I had a very sort of slender technique. I wasn't a great technician at all and to be cast opposite him was terribly exciting but I was very apprehensive. You see, the minute I walked on set for the rehearsal, we had one working light and a piano player. He was so dear and knew full well, I imagine, being a sensitive man, how I felt. But he was fun, made me relax and before you knew it there was some music going and he says, 'Let's try a few steps, and off we went."[38]

In 1957, Fred wrote to Audrey in a letter, saying, "They just simply say 'It's the Best Musical Ever Made!' That's from the wise ones too. They rave over you and your dancing [ . . . ] In all my experience with musical pictures I have never experienced such a reaction from people. Now, I see no reason why the public should not fall for it too."[39] Production for *Funny Face* finally concluded in Paris in early July. To celebrate, the Ferrers threw a party for the cast and crew on a bateau-mouche (a river cruise boat that sails along the Seine) with a musical band in tow. Audrey wore a Givenchy pale pink silk taffeta dress in the popular chemise style. *Funny Face* had been a taxing production. To recover from the long days, Audrey returned to Switzerland for a short recess before reporting back to Paris in August for her next film, *Love in the Afternoon*, directed by Billy Wilder. ✳

# { 5 }
# Hôtel
# Raphaël

Since their wedding in 1954 Audrey and Mel had become professional nomads. Over the next few years they would success-fully master the art of living out of their suitcases to accommodate their active work schedules. As Audrey explained, "Mel and I really have no home, no home at all except a tiny cottage in Switzerland. We're always on the move—in New York, France, in Hollywood and in Lucerne and in Germany."[40] After marrying, Audrey and Mel divided their time between two rental homes: a small chalet in Bürgenstock, Switzerland (near Lac Lucerne) and an Italian villa in the Alban Hills outside of Rome. It wasn't until 1963 that the couple settled down in Tolochenaz, a small village in Switzerland. *La Paisible*, "The Peaceful," was an eighteenth-century farmhouse on a large acreage of land surrounded by orchards. Blissfully tucked away at *La Paisible*, Audrey could escape the trivial demands of celeb-ritydom and bask in the stillness of the Swiss Alps. Yet, before purchasing her Swiss hideaway, the Ferrers shuffled between rental properties, friends' houses, and hotels. One place they considered a surrogate home was the Hôtel Raphaël in Paris. Their permanent suite was room 312.

The Hôtel Raphaël was founded by Léonard Tauber and Constant Baverez in 1925 and designed by architect André Rousselot. The hotel, located on avenue Kléber in the Sixteenth Arrondissement of Paris, was named after the Italian painter and archi-tect Raphaël. Tauber, known for his intimate and more personal establishments, wanted to create a modest yet exclusive luxury hotel reserved for elite clientele. The Hôtel Raphaël is composed of forty-seven rooms and thirty-six suites, some over-looking the desirable cityscape views of the Eiffel Tower and the Arc de Triomphe. The rooms are spacious with high ceilings, many of which are inter-connected, but most impressive is the rooftop terrace with panoramic views of the Paris skyline. The fash-ionable hotel is handsomely dressed in Parisian furnishings and dark oak paneling. The bedrooms and living areas are decorated with antique Louis XV and Louis XVI furniture that beautifully complement the hotel's traditional decor. The Raphaël has had an impressive guest list including regulars such as Cary Grant, Katharine Hepburn, Ava Gardner, Billy Wilder, and Ingrid Bergman. In fact, it was at the Hôtel Raphaël where Audrey and Ingrid Bergman were first introduced. Audrey and Mel were newlyweds residing at the Raphaël when they bumped into Ingrid, who was also a guest at the Parisian hotspot. Audrey regarded Ingrid as one of the greatest actresses in the world. The two women immediately hit it off and became steadfast friends. In 1956, Mel and Ingrid would film the movie *Elena et les Hommes* in Paris and in December of that year Audrey and Mel would attend the French adaptation of the stage play *Tea and Sympathy* starring Miss Bergman in Paris.

During most of 1956, Audrey occupied room 312 while she was in town filming *Funny Face* and *Love in the Afternoon*. It was difficult to achieve a sense of stability with the Ferrers' nonstop lifestyles, but checking into the same suite felt like home. After years of traveling, Audrey found it challenging trying to balance her work and home life. Yet globe-trotting did have its perks and over the years she had perfected the technique of suitcase living: "I suppose I get tired of packing and unpacking, but actually I'm loving it all. I'm an expert packer by now, and we have a system. We send the heavy stuff on ahead by ship, then we send other things by air freight and take our personal things on the plane with us, and that definitely includes my amazing Yorkshire terrier. It's called Famous of Assam and goes everywhere with us."[41] Audrey had an aptitude for organization and was fastidious about packing and sorting their belongings. "In addition to quickly handling correspondence and responding to invitations," Mel said of his wife, "she is adept at setting up a home wherever she is. It is as if, like a magician, she pulled everything out of a hat. She just needs a certain number of suitcases."[42]

On arrival at the Raphaël, Audrey took it upon herself to redecorate their room. She prided herself on being a good housewife and was determined to create a cozier atmosphere for her and her husband. Her only critique was that the radiators weren't hot enough to cook on. Within seconds of their arrival, Audrey would swiftly begin removing any item that bore the hotel's name. She would replace the ashtrays and pamphlets with personal touches, such as her silver candlesticks, picture frames, her own set of pillows and linens, books, a record player, and record albums. She would hang artwork on the walls, like the paintings she and Mel collected by the young French artists Jean Pierre Capron and Bernard Buffet. Never one to waste time, Audrey would begin unpacking and rearranging the furniture with the help of the hotel staff. She would personally move items around until the room was exactly how she desired. On one occasion, she called the concierge to request a small table that had been in her room during their previous stay. The concierge apologetically explained that the table was now in another suite, but Audrey insisted and she got her wish. Moments later the table arrived at her door.

Although, the Ferrers favored the accommodations at the Raphaël, they would occasionally find excuses to stay at other Parisian hotels like the popular Ritz Hotel on 5 Place Vendôme or the Hôtel Lancaster near the Champs-Elysées, where she stayed while filming *Two for the Road*. As Audrey's lifestyle began to change so did her living arrangements. In 1962, while shooting *Paris When It Sizzles* and *Charade*, Audrey made the more sensible decision and rented a large château just outside of Fontainebleau. She was now the mother of a two-year-old son, Sean, and the confinements of a cramped hotel suite were no longer practical for her growing family. However, for many years, it was the Hôtel Raphaël that provided her with the comforts of home, especially during her early honeymoon years. ✳

OPPOSITE Audrey and Mel in their suite at the Hôtel Raphaël in Paris,1956.

# { 6 }
# Love in the Afternoon

Audrey's schedule left little time for relaxation; shortly after production wrapped on *Funny Face*, she redirected her attention to her next film. *Love in the Afternoon*, loosely based on the novel *Ariane, Jeune Fille Russe* by Claude Anet, reunited Audrey with her *Sabrina* director, Billy Wilder. This time the two were joined by Gary Cooper and Maurice Chevalier in Paris for the romantic comedy produced by Allied Artists. Ariane Chavasse (Audrey) is a young cellist who lives at home with her father (Maurice Chevalier), a private detective, in their quaint Paris apartment. Ariane is intrigued by her father's cases and becomes enamored by one of his regulars, an urbane American playboy, Frank Flannagan (Gary Cooper), who she innocently pursues with wild stories about her invented love affairs. Production was originally set for February of 1956, but due to scheduling conflicts by the three principal actors, filming was postponed until August. Prior to filming, Audrey spent twelve days learning how to convincingly play a cello from a former member of the Philharmonie de Paris at his pied-à-terre located on the left bank of the Seine. Additionally, the studio organized two unusual appointments for their lead actress. They arranged a weekend for Audrey to train with a trapeze artist from Cirque d'Hiver for a scene where her character had to scale the outer wall of the Hôtel Ritz. They also had Audrey attend private lessons to learn a few bullfighting moves so she could do a takeoff on a matador.

The Ferrers arrived in Paris in August 1956 and, once again, took residence at the Hôtel Raphaël. Early into their relationship, Audrey and Mel agreed that they would choose projects that were in close proximity to each other. While Audrey was busy at work with *Love in the Afternoon* at the Studios de Boulogne, a film studio on the southern end of the Bois de Boulogne, Mel was filming *The Vintage* at Joinville Studios on the opposite end of Paris. Soon, the cast and crew of *The Vintage* would leave for Saint-Tropez. Audrey would call Mel nightly and they would frequently see each other on weekends. "Mel and I have been rather crafty planning so that we can be both filming together in Paris," Audrey explained. "We are both booked now with film roles until June next year."[43] The Ferrers were enjoying their lives as newlyweds. Like clockwork, every evening after a long day of shooting, Mel would meet Audrey at the Studios de Boulogne and together they would walk the three-mile trek along the Bois de Boulogne back to their hotel.

Before production began, Audrey was already making headlines. She had recently cut her hair for *Love in the Afternoon* and her new coiffure was quite the departure from her popular pixie cut. Audrey's hairstyles had been a source of conversation since

ABOVE TOP Audrey and Mel in front of the Eiffel Tower.
ABOVE BOTTOM Audrey at a cafe in Paris. OPPOSITE
Audrey at Gambais Lake (Château de Vitry in the
background) during the filming of *Love in the Afternoon*.

her Italian cut in *Roman Holiday* and for the last
year she had been steadily growing out her hair.
Audrey's new hairstyle, appropriately named "Paris
Heart," was created and first done by American
hairdresser Kenneth Battelle (aka Mr. Kenneth).
Under Mr. Kenneth's instructions, the Paris Heart
was then re-created in Paris by famed French hairstylist Alexandre de Paris, who styled Audrey's
coiffure for the opera scene in *Love in the Afternoon*
and publicity photos. However, the person responsible for Audrey's tresses during filming was her
hairdresser Grazia de Rossi. During the production
of *War and Peace*, Audrey's hair and makeup team
was an Italian married couple, Alberto and Grazia
de Rossi. Audrey felt an immediate familial connection to the Rossis and hired them to style her for
*Love in the Afternoon*. They would continue to work
together for the majority of her career. The Paris
Heart was a neck-length haircut with a center part
and soft waves that gently tucked around the face.
Critics raved about her new, youthful hairstyle, but
Audrey was most concerned about her husband's
impression: "I've always paid a great deal of attention to the styling of my hair because it's not an
interesting color. It's straight as pump water but
monstrously thick, so it takes to different styles
easily. I like change. I think a new hair-do does the
same thing for a woman that a new hat does. One
certainly wouldn't want to wear the same hat all
the time! Of course, husbands are a hazard. They
always loathe anything different for the first week,
and then they get used to it and are quite happy."[44]

Audrey wouldn't have to wait long for Mel's
reaction. On August 25, Mel was given a day leave
from *The Vintage*, which was filming in Nice, to
visit Audrey in Paris to celebrate his thirty-ninth
birthday. Audrey was all smiles when she greeted
her husband at the airport. It was Mel's first time
seeing Audrey's fresh cut and he was smitten.
Billy Wilder, Gary Cooper, and Maurice Chevalier
cohosted a birthday dinner for Mel at the Studios

de Boulogne. But dessert was reserved for Audrey. After dinner, the Ferrers retreated to their hotel room, where Audrey presented her husband with a chocolate birthday cake prepared by a private chef. In the privacy of their suite, Audrey gifted Mel a platinum Rolex watch engraved MAD ABOUT THE MAN, a nod to the song by Noël Coward.

By this time, Audrey and Hubert de Givenchy had worked successfully on two movies (*Sabrina* and *Funny Face*). So once again, Audrey requested, and the studio sanctioned, Hubert to design the costumes for her character, Ariane. The two collaborators were confident about the pieces they selected for *Love in the Afternoon*. The wardrobe for Ariane needed to emphasize a simplicity and youthfulness that was indicative of the character's innocent nature. Audrey spent five afternoons with Hubert at his Paris atelier choosing models from his latest couture collection and boutique line. Based off their discussions, Hubert made special modifications to reflect Audrey's personal taste. "When I came to Paris, I went to several fashion shows and

found Paris fashions pretty and sophisticated. But when I saw the collection of Hubert de Givenchy I felt he would make the clothes that most suited me," Audrey said to reporter Nora Martin during the making of *Love in the Afternoon*. "I think he uses extreme looking models to show a new trend and then follows it up with clothes in more simple styles based on this 'shock-line.'"[45]

Together they decided on eleven outfits (totaling $35,000), which included a mixture of separates and dresses that perfectly encapsulated Parisian elegance. Coincidentally, Audrey had been eyed for the role of Cécile for the Hollywood adaptation of

ABOVE Audrey wearing her black shantung Givenchy dress inside her dressing room at the Studios de Boulogne.
OPPOSITE Audrey and Gary Cooper filming inside the "Ritz Paris" on a soundstage at the Studios de Boulogne.

*Bonjour Tristesse*, based on the novel by Françoise Sagan. For reasons concerning the character's morality, Audrey turned down *Bonjour Tristesse* and, in turn, accepted the role of Ariane. Yet it was Givenchy who was hired to create the costumes for both films. Adopting designs from his most recent collection, Ariane's and Cécile's costumes were similar in fabric and pattern but with contrasting silhouettes. Audrey chose a higher neckline and longer hemline, whereas the actress playing Cécile, Jean Seberg, preferred a halter cut and shorter skirts.

One of Ariane's looks was composed of a black shantung dress with a shallow neck, full skirt, and a wide, stiff bow that swept along the length of the neckline. This dress was made exclusively for Audrey with fabric from Givenchy's Spring collection. Suitable for the opera, Audrey wore an exquisite strapless white point d'esprit organdy

gown with scallop neckline. Embroidered along the chest and hemline were touches of turquoise, silver threading, beaded florets, and rhinestones. Accentuating her delicate waistline and adding a dash of color sat a single turquoise satin bow. Hubert paired the dress with a white silk bolero jacket and opera gloves. Audrey also wore two floral print dresses created specifically for Ariane's wardrobe. The first was a cocktail dress made of white organdy with a threaded floral motif and a bateau neckline with a small bow at the waist. The second was a sleeveless day dress of white silk printed with small roses and two bows tied in the back. For a more casual ensemble, better suited for an outdoor picnic, Audrey wore a red cardigan, white blouse, and red-and-blue-striped cigarette pants with three buttons clasped just above the ankle. To complement the occasion, she wore

her hair in pigtails tied with matching red bows. Hubert's designs perfectly embodied the demure persona of both Audrey and Ariane, adding a fashionable layer to Audrey's performance.

Production began in late August in 1956 at the Studios de Boulogne on the rue de Silly in Paris. Unlike *Funny Face*, which spent a month shooting at numerous outdoor locations, *Love in the Afternoon* was mostly shot on a soundstage. Wilder had originally planned to shoot the film in Hollywood but at the behest of his lead actors, all who had prior commitments in Europe, he moved the production to France. Wilder worked with a French crew and stuck to French hours: noon to 7:30 P.M. The interior shots were filmed entirely at the Studios de Boulogne, at the direction of production designer Alexandre Trauner, who with his crew, built exact replicas of the Conservatory of Music and the Ritz

ABOVE TOP Audrey with makeup artist Alberto de Rossi and Maurice Chevalier on the set of *Love in the Afternoon*. ABOVE BOTTOM Audrey with Mel, Maurice Chevalier, and Fernandel at a cocktail party. OPPOSITE Audrey photographed on the streets of Paris during her off hours.

Hotel, re-creating the suites, halls, corridors, and foyer down to the most minute detail.

Although the majority of scenes were filmed at the Studios de Boulogne, Audrey and Gary (or "Mr. Coop" as Audrey called him) were treated to a romantic picnic filmed outside Château de Vitry. Château de Vitry was a nineteenth-century castle in Gambais about thirty miles south of Paris. The cast and crew spent four days filming Audrey and Gary chomping on chicken legs and rowing a boat along Gambais Lake. The location was lush, picturesque, and, unfortunately for Billy Wilder, full of wildlife.

The simple scene, which shouldn't have taken long to film, was repeatedly interrupted by chickens, ducks, and airplanes buzzing overhead. Wilder and his soundmen couldn't hide their frustrations. Everyone was ready to give up until Gary Cooper noticed that every time Wilder blew his horn to signal action, the noise reverberating from the instrument resembled a duck call, igniting the relentless quacking. Wilder retired his horn and recommended filming. Surprisingly, after watching the rushes, Wilder made an unexpected decision. "Say, that's fine!" he said. "Keep those ducks in. Sounds kinda ironic."[46]

However, for the two lead actors, the constant disturbance meant they were forced to eat dozens of chicken legs. After a fresh basket was placed on the table, a glum Audrey exclaimed she couldn't look at another drumstick. Thankfully, the inconvenience didn't dampen their spirits and the two leads enjoyed their time together on the lake. Audrey, wearing her hair in pigtails, entertained Gary by imitating a matador. Putting to use the moves she had learned prior to production, Audrey wore a breadbasket on her head and held a tablecloth near her body pretending it was a muleta. She enchanted the cast and crew, imagining the baguette was a sword and performing her bullfighting moves as Gary watched in amusement.

Regardless of Audrey's busy filming schedule, she maintained a healthy social calendar during her time in Paris. On September 5, Richard Avedon photographed Audrey for the October cover of *Harper's Bazaar*. She modeled a collection of new Parisian hats, including a zebra print beret by John Frederick styled with a pair of Cartier coral flower earrings. Later that month, Audrey received an unexpected invitation from American author Ernest Hemingway. A close friend of Gary Cooper, Hemingway was also in

ABOVE Audrey and Mel, photographed by Zinn Arthur, celebrating Mel's thirty-ninth birthday at the Hôtel Raphaël.

Paris and insisted on meeting the young actress. He had just seen Audrey in *War and Peace* and made plans with Audrey and Mel for an evening of fun. On September 29, Audrey, Gary Cooper, and actress Marlene Dietrich attended a performance by Maurice Chevalier at the Alhambra, where he performed his nightly revue.

There was lots of fun to be had on the set of *Love in the Afternoon*. Henry Fonda, Audrey's costar in *War and Peace*, made an impromptu visit and spent the day on set with the Ferrers. On October 15, a reception was held at the Studios de Boulogne for the cast and crew. In attendance were French actors Fernandel and Charles Vanel. The Gypsy orchestra, hired by Billy Wilder for the movie, performed a concert for the partygoers and played "Fascination Waltz," a song heavily featured in *Love in the Afternoon*. To everyone's surprise, Audrey and Mel danced to the Castle waltz as guests enjoyed petits fours and refreshments.

On November 16, Audrey and Mel, accompanied by Gary Cooper, Maurice Chevalier, and Billy Wilder, flew to London to attend the British premiere of *War and Peace* at the Plaza Theatre in London. They were there for less than twenty-four hours before returning to Paris the following morning. Unfortunately, production was delayed after Cooper and Wilder fell ill. Gary was holed up in his hotel room recovering from the flu; meanwhile, Billy Wilder took time off to nurse a cold and a bad case of kidney stones. "It was the Paris weather," she reasoned. "We had to wear summer clothes and it was very cold."[47] Audrey was one of the few who didn't get sick.

The final scene in *Love in the Afternoon* was shot at Gare de Lyon, a railway station located in the Twelfth Arrondissement in the east of Paris. The crew spent three days filming at platform 5. Audrey and Gary filmed their tearful goodbyes as commuters walked along the platform making their regular connections. The three principal leads were given their own train compartment as substitute dressing rooms. Audrey spent her downtime in her carriage, collecting herself, as she prepared for her final scene in which she had to cry. Audrey's makeup artist, Alberto de Rossi, sprayed glycerin on Audrey's cheeks to replicate teardrops.

Paris, known for its unstable weather patterns, was unexpectedly sunny that day, which made filming difficult. The scene was meant to be gray and melancholy but the persistent blue skies were complicating production. Billy Wilder made the quick decision to install screens and water down the platform to create a gloomier atmosphere. In the final scene, an emotional Ariane accompanies Frank Flannagan to the train station as he prepares to leave Paris. Frank, overcome by Ariane's tearful state, finally submits to his feelings and pulls her onto the train as she calls out "I'll be all right!" In true Hollywood fashion, Frank and Ariane kiss as the train departs the station. *Love in the Afternoon* wrapped in December.

Audrey treasured her time filming *Love in the Afternoon* but friends were concerned about the exhausted actress. Her nonstop filming schedule left Audrey overworked with little time for recovery. However, Audrey and Mel had already made a commitment in New York. The two left Paris to begin rehearsals for their live, on-air television movie, *Mayerling*, which aired in the United States on February 4, 1957. Audrey returned to Paris briefly in January of 1958 at the request of her newest director, Fred Zinneman. She had signed on to star in the upcoming Warner Brothers' picture, *The Nun's Story*. Zinneman had arranged for his lead actresses to stay at various convents in Paris for several days and embrace the life of a nun. It was mid-January and blistering cold, but Audrey approached her assignment with the seriousness of a devout student. As she recounted to journalist Angela Fox Dunn of *The Gazette*, "[Zinnemann] took me to convents and left me there for twenty-four hours at a time. I slept in a cell and got up at 4:00 A.M. to pray on the ice-cold stone floor. And I was totally secluded. Only the mother superior knew. She had to give permission."[48]

Between 1956 and 1962 Audrey continued to visit Paris for fashion shows, dress fittings, photo shoots, and the one-off stay at the convent; but it would be another six years after *Love in the Afternoon* before she returned to Paris to film her next movie, *Paris When It Sizzles*. ✳

# { 7 }
# Mr. Famous and Assam

In 1956, while in Paris for *Funny Face*, the Ferrers introduced a new member to their family, a five-pound Yorkshire terrier named Mr. Famous. Mel had purchased the small terrier from a pet shop in Paris as a gift for his wife. This came as a pleasant surprise to Audrey, who confessed, "I never thought I'd get a dog until Mel said one day, 'I think you need a dog.' Then I telephoned the Paris kennel from St. Moritz, and they told me they had this wonderful Yorkshire terrier. I've always loved animals. I take it around in a basket with a cushion and in a canvas shopping bag."[49] Actress Elizabeth Taylor and director Billy Wilder's wife, Audrey Wilder, were also clients of the popular Paris breeder. Liz's Yorkshire terrier was named Assam Lady Puff and Audrey Wilder's was named Fifty.

Since her childhood Audrey had longed to be a mother. "When I was little, I used to embarrass my mother by trying to pick babies out of prams at the market. The one thing I dreamed of in my life was to have children of my own."[50] Sadly, after her first miscarriage in March of 1955, Audrey's dream felt further out of reach. So, when Mel broached the idea of welcoming a new addition to the family, Audrey jumped in delight. Mr. Famous, or Famous as he was commonly known, quickly filled Audrey's

maternal void. The two were inseparable. Famous would become her constant companion and a proficient traveler, crossing the Atlantic on numerous occasions. But his favorite mode of transportation was in the handlebar basket of Audrey's bicycle. The heads at Paramount were so taken by the adoring duo they created a special lever for Audrey's bicycle that attached a front basket so Audrey could transport Famous around the studio lot.

OPPOSITE Audrey with Assam on the Warner Bros lot during the production of *My Fair Lady*, 1963. ABOVE Audrey with Famous at the Ciampino airport in Rome, 1958.

In a family full of actors, it seemed only fitting that Famous would try his hand at showbiz. He made his acting debut in *Love in the Afternoon*. He spent nearly two weeks on set filming his scenes and never missed his mark. (It should be noted, the small terrier used in *Funny Face* was a doppelgänger.) Mr. Famous was a regular on Audrey's movie sets and patiently sat on a chair or cushion waiting for Audrey to finish her scenes. In the afternoon, the two would enjoy a cup of tea in her dressing room before returning to work. Like his mother, Famous was an experienced flyer. Audrey made special arrangements for him to accompany her in the Belgian Congo while she

ABOVE LEFT Audrey and Assam on the set of *Charade* in Paris, 1962. ABOVE RIGHT Audrey with Famous in the Belgian Congo during the production of *The Nun's Story*, 1958.

filmed *The Nun's Story*. He traveled to Paris, Rome, Hollywood, and New York, where Audrey shot *Breakfast at Tiffany's*. In New York, the happy duo would stroll through Central Park during their downtime. Very often, effusive passersby would stop Audrey to admire her teacup terrier, totally oblivious of his famous mother.

The pampered pup was accustomed to only the best: steak dinners, five-star hotels, and lots of love and affection. He quickly adapted to hotel living and had zero issues finding his new rooms; but he was a mischievous one. He had a proclivity for snatching the mail left outside each hotel suite when he would make his way down the corridor. Thankfully, his mother would personally return the letters to their rightful owners.

Just like Audrey, he always looked his best. He was perfectly groomed and never without a bow tied around a tuft of fur on top of his petite head. His accessories were carefully chosen and often matched his mother's ensembles. However, the little guy was a nervous pooch and would sometimes misbehave, especially in the presence of other dogs. "This feller has delusions of grandeur when he sees a big dog," Audrey shared with Harold Heffernan of the North American Newspaper Alliance. "He thinks he's a lion. The rest of the time he thinks he is a small person. He'd be broken hearted if he ever discovered that he is just a small dog."[51]

Mr. Famous sadly passed away in 1961, when Audrey was in Los Angeles filming *The Children's Hour*. He wandered off into traffic on Sunset Boulevard and was hit by a car. Audrey was devastated by the passing of her small companion. The loss of Famous left her heartbroken. She retreated to Paris with Mel and their newborn son, Sean, to distance herself from the tragic memory. In Paris, Mel presented her with a new Yorkshire Terrier, Assam of Assam. The name Assam came from the Sanskrit word for "uneven" because of his slightly crooked features.

Assam would ease the overbearing heaviness left by his predecessor. He quickly became Audrey's little confidant. Like Famous, he would also become a capable jet-setter. The two would travel internationally to movie sets, fashion shoots, and film premieres. He appeared in many promotional photos with his mother, never resisting the spotlight. He traveled to Paris for *Paris When It Sizzles*, *Charade*, *How to Steal a Million*, and *Two for the Road*. The adoring crew members would fawn over Audrey's diminutive protector. As with Famous, Audrey would also teach Assam to sit patiently while his mother worked, certain to never disturb the filming process. He, too, would make himself at home in Audrey's handlebar basket, zooming across the Warner Brothers lot during the production of *My Fair Lady*.

Another, more expensive form of transportation was in one of Audrey's specially made Louis Vuitton bags. Audrey was a longtime client of the French luxury house. Once her career began to take off, Audrey became an avid customer and purchased a small set of luggage in 1955, during her three-day work trip in Paris. Over the years she would continue to frequent their stores, acquiring quite the collection. One of their most popular purses was the Speedy; crafted of coated canvas, the bag was designed to fold up and fit in a suitcase convenient for air travel. At the time the bag came in three sizes: 30, 35, and 40. Audrey was a fan of the popular travel bag but saw room for improvement. In 1965, she contacted Louis Vuitton and requested a smaller version of the Speedy, one for everyday use, hence the Speedy 25 was born. Audrey carried the compact bag everywhere and was often photographed in airports lugging her suitcases and her nifty Speedy 25. At one point, Louis Vuitton made a special version of the Speedy for their loyal client. They produced a larger size that had one side made of transparent plastic with holes for ventilation. Now Audrey could safely and stylishly travel with her miniature pooch wherever she went, whether it was Paris, Rome, New York, or Switzerland.

Famous and Assam would always hold a special place in Audrey's heart. For years, Audrey lived a hectic lifestyle. She did not occupy a permanent address and spent the majority of her time traveling for work. Her Yorkshire terriers provided her with unconditional love and a sense of security that she had yearned for since childhood: "I think an animal, especially a dog, is possibly the purest experience you can have. No person and few children, unless they're still infants, are as unpremeditated, as undemanding, really. They only ask to survive. They want to eat. They are totally dependent on you, and therefore completely vulnerable. And this complete vulnerability is what enables you to open your heart completely, which you rarely do to a human being. Except, perhaps, children. Who thinks you're as fantastic as your dog?"[52] ✳

# { 8 }

# Paris Fashion Week

In the summer of 1959, style enthusiasts gathered in the fashion capital for the unveiling of Paris's most coveted haute couture collections. Paris Fashion Week was treated as a sacred event among socialites and fashion insiders. Loyal clients cleared their schedules and gleefully filled the salons of Paris's premier designers with their checkbooks in hand. Throngs of elegantly dressed women excitedly discussed their predictions as they made their way toward their seats sandwiched between journalists and buyers. Among the in vogue crowd was Audrey Hepburn and her husband, Mel Ferrer. The Ferrers were often seen at Paris fashion shows. Always seated next to each other, the two would attentively take notes about the exquisite garments that passed their direction. The couple shared a mutual appreciation for clothes. Where most men encouraged their wives to shop alone, Mel had a vested interest in his wife's wardrobe and paid careful attention to Audrey's image. He accompanied Audrey to various fashion shows (even opting to go alone when Audrey was too busy) and would offer his opinion at her dress fittings.

Edith Head, chief costume designer at Paramount, noted that Audrey would take home sketch designs to Mel before making any final decisions.

Audrey was the first to admit that she relied on Mel's judgment: "He is very aware of my clothes and very firm about how he wants me to look. He doesn't compromise. He has good taste and a very good eye for line. He dresses well himself and he knows what's good for me."[53]

Audrey knew the impact fashion had on her career. Her style choices had become a significant part of her identity on- and off-screen. Following her prosperous collaboration with Hubert de Givenchy in *Sabrina*, she was quickly propelled into the world of haute couture and high fashion. From a young age she exhibited a keen eye for styling and instinctively knew how to dress for her figure. "I love fashion. I know the school of thought exists that you should basically always wear the same line. The one you have chosen as the best for you. But the fun of clothes for me is the change. I am enjoying the short skirts, the empire waistline and the gay, blown-out look," Audrey told beauty columnist Lydia Lane in 1959. She continued, "Learning how to dress is expensive but your mistakes are your best teacher. When I wear a dress that I know is not right for me—no matter how expensive it is—I give it away. I don't want to be tempted to wear something that's unbecoming."[54]

Being a public figure had its drawbacks, especially for Audrey, who was a self-confessed introvert. Her clothes were like her armor; they instilled her with confidence when she was in front of a camera

OPPOSITE Audrey and Mel Ferrer at the Dior fashion show.

or on a red carpet. However, clothes could also have a "devastating effect" on her personality if she felt uncomfortable in her attire. "My conversation and even my enjoyment of being with people are affected," she acknowledged. "There is something magic about a beautifully made dress and no substitute for exquisite detail, a perfect fit, a fine fabric. You can wear it season after season with a confident feeling of being well dressed."[55] Although Audrey trusted the designs of Hubert de Givenchy, she loved the playfulness of dressing up and experimenting with different designers. During the last few days of July in 1959, Audrey attended two shows by fashion pantheons Chanel and Dior.

The first show Audrey attended was the Chanel fashion show given on July 29 at Coco Chanel's salon at 31 rue Cambon. Chanel's shows were regarded as a national event in the French capital. Her modern take on women's clothing reshaped the world of fashion and redefined the way women dressed. Diana Vreeland, fashion editor at *Harper's Bazaar*, was an ardent admirer of the French couturier and praised her chic simplicity; "No one had a better sense of luxury than Coco Chanel. She really had the spirit of the twentieth century."[56] After a fifteen-year retirement from the industry, Chanel reemerged in 1954 to great acclaim, and her 1959 Summer collection was receiving glowing reviews from the press. Returning to the ranks, Madame Chanel presented her classic suit with a slight twist on tradition. She described her new collection as "more brilliant than usual, younger, and full of surprises."[57] Her tweed suits retained their classic straight fit with trademark piping, flat collars, and outer patch pockets. However, the jackets and sleeves were shortened with the hemlines worn just below the knee. The suits were presented in scrumptious colors such as mauve, pink, orange, lettuce green, and navy blue.

OPPOSITE Audrey, Mel, and Richard Avedon with Coco Chanel at her pied-à-terre after the Chanel fashion show.

Models paraded around in long tunic dresses with three-quarter-length sleeves and slits on either side of the skirt revealing a slim matching underskirt. Chanel draped her willowy mannequins in strings of pearls and structured berets that were strategically placed on the back of their heads.

Audrey was prominently positioned in the front row corner with Mel seated in the chair behind her. She wore an off-white Givenchy waistless linen dress complemented by soft makeup and her hair worn down, straight and parted in the middle. The Ferrers held hands during the show, and Audrey affectionately brushed her hand against Mel's cheek. When asked if she would buy anything form Chanel's Summer collection, Audrey answered, "This is the first show I've seen this season. I don't know yet whether I'll buy a lot of new clothes. I'm waiting to see what they're like."[58]

Audrey and Mel had a hard time containing their enthusiasm. They whispered to each other each time a dress caught their attention. Audrey would discreetly signal to Mel which garment she liked and he would quietly scribble the item number on a piece of paper. They both showed delight when a model wearing a waistless brocade evening dress walked down the aisle. "That's very pretty—Divine!"[59] she exclaimed. Audrey was more attentive than usual. She was covertly selecting pieces for her next project. Seated next to the Ferrers was their friend, fashion photographer Richard Avedon. Audrey and Avedon (whom she had worked with on *Funny Face*) were collaborating on a deliciously fun fashion editorial slated for *Harper's Bazaar*'s September issue. The photo shoot was scheduled for next month in Paris.

Ensconced at the top of a long marble staircase, Coco Chanel scrutinized her creations through the curved mirrors that lined the walls leading to her apartment. When the fashion show concluded, Chanel retreated from her secure spot and joined her guests upstairs at her private

residence. She was dressed in her typical uniform: a beige Chanel suit, a brimmed hat, and coils of pearls strung around her neck. In 1918, Chanel had purchased the entire building on 31 rue Cambon. She'd transformed the building, originally built after the French Revolution, into her atelier and private pied-à-terre. Famously averse to doors, Chanel furnished her apartment with antique Coromandel screens and walls of bookshelves filled with leather-bound tomes. Her custom-made crystal chandeliers hung from the ceiling, drawing the eye upward. Beneath the dazzling focal point was a handsome suede camel-colored couch that faced out to a selection of silk fauteuil chairs.

PREVIOUS Audrey and Mel at the Dior fashion show. ABOVE Audrey and Mel with Coco Chanel and Marie-Louise Bousquet, Paris Editor at *Harper's Bazaar*, after the Chanel show.

After the show, Audrey, Mel, and Avedon joined Coco Chanel upstairs to congratulate her on her latest achievement. They discussed potential pieces for the *Harper's Bazaar* editorial and the possibility of incorporating Chanel's white wool coat with black silk braid lined in curly lamb worn over a matching tunic dress.

The following day, Audrey and Mel arrived at the Dior fashion show on avenue Montaigne. It was a delicate time at Dior. Following the death of Christian Dior in October 1957, Dior's young protégé, Yves Saint Laurent, had become his successor and artistic director of the haute couture fashion house at the tender age of twenty-one. Saint Laurent had begun his career at Dior in 1955 after completing his studies at the École de la Chambre Syndicale de la Haute Couture. In the beginning, Saint Laurent had managed menial tasks as he worked his way up the Dior ladder. It was evident early on that Saint Laurent was a gifted artist and at the encouragement of his mentor, he submitted his sketches for future collections. Christian Dior nurtured his protégé's talents and began incorporating Saint Laurent's designs into his own shows.

Shortly after Christian Dior's death in 1957, the house of Dior announced Yves Saint Laurent as their new head designer, making him the world's youngest couturier. His first showcase for Dior's 1958 Spring Summer collection was an instant triumph met by a standing ovation from elated fanatics. Like his predecessor, Saint Laurent wanted to reinvent the way women dressed and thus introduced the Trapeze Line. It was a daring departure from Dior's signature style; Saint Laurent abandoned the cinch waist for a fresher and more simplified silhouette. His inaugural collection was universally lauded and a financial success for the renowned fashion house. However, his second launch for his 1958 Autumn Winter collection wasn't met with the same enthusiasm. His "New New Look" consisting of long, outdated hemlines was disparaged by the press and left Saint Laurent on thin ice.

Yet, on July 30, 1959, only two days before Saint Laurent's twenty-third birthday, Dior's atelier on avenue Montaigne was teeming in anticipation for the premiere of his Winter show. The salon was overflowing with hopeful guests, so much so that Audrey and Mel were unable to reach their seats. They were led outside through a separate entrance to the salon and escorted to their chairs in the front row. Audrey was dressed in a pale blue Givenchy wool sleeveless dress with her hair slicked back in a tight bun and minimal makeup. Once more, she was seated in the front row corner spot with Mel situated behind her. Yves Saint Laurent made a bold statement in his newest collection; he raised the hemlines above the kneecap, creating a stir among the fashion world. The audience was left silent but Audrey shared her thrill at the radical new trend: "I'm all for short skirts—even to the kneecap if you've got the right legs."[60]

Saint Laurent's Winter collection centered on the length of his hemlines, which he proclaimed was the secret to his collection. His *puff* skirt was the centerpiece of the show. His dresses were presented in wool and silk and belted at the waist with a bell shape skirt that cinched above the knee, creating a tiered effect that tapered off above the kneecap. Suits in wool, mohair, tweed, and plaids were paired with short jackets, some belted and some loose, fitted with skirts that fell above or below the knee. The models wore large earrings, layered choker necklaces, and felt wool and fur toque hats. Audrey took special notice of the avant-garde designs. Like the Chanel show, she was there to select garments for her *Harper's Bazaar* photo shoot titled "Paris Pursuit." Of the designs, Audrey chose four pieces to wear including a puffed tunic sleeveless dress in a Moreau tweed of dark blue with matching jacket.

Audrey and Mel were visibly pleased by the beautiful creations shown at the Dior and Chanel salons. The past two days had been a successful outing and together with Richard Avedon, Audrey felt confident about the clothes she chose for *Harper's Bazaar*. ✳

# Harper's Bazaar—
# Paris Pursuit

In August of 1959, Audrey joined Richard Avedon and some familiar faces on the restless streets of Paris for *Harper's Bazaar*'s fashion editorial titled "Paris Pursuit." This was certainly not the first time Audrey had collaborated with the revered photographer; her earliest memory of Avedon dated back to 1951, when she was plucked from obscurity and landed the lead role in Broadway's *Gigi*. At that time, producer Gilbert Miller had arranged for two important photo shoots for his sprightly ingénue: one with Irving Penn for *Vogue* magazine and the second with American fashion photographer Richard Avedon. Coming directly from London by boat, Audrey arrived in New York City for the first time with a stomach full of butterflies. She was quickly whisked away to Avedon's studio, where she donned her Gigi costume and nervously posed before Avedon's electrifying camera. "The first thing I saw when I came to America was the Statue of Liberty. The second—Richard Avedon," Audrey fondly recalled during her speech at the 1989 CFDA (Council of Fashion Designers of America) tribute to Richard Avedon. "Before I knew it, I was in front of Avedon's cameras, lights flashing, music going,

FLOWERS:
IN FASHION
IN ART
IN BEAUTY

60 cents

---

OPPOSITE Audrey, Mel, and Richard Avedon, photographed by Henry Wolf, on the set of the *Paris Pursuit* fashion shoot. ABOVE Audrey on the cover of *Harper's Bazaar*, April 1956.

Richard snapping away a mile a minute, darting from one angle to the other like a hummingbird, everywhere at once, weaving his spell."[61]

Audrey's portrait by Avedon appeared on the cover of *Theatre Arts* magazine in February 1952. She was wearing a navy blue nautical dress with matching hat inspired by the dresses Colette wore during her teenage years. Soon after, draped in an off-the-shoulder buttercup yellow gown by Ceil

Chapman, a twenty-two-year-old Audrey is perched on a ladder in front of a blooming yellow mimosa tree. The fanciful photo by Avedon was featured in *Harper's Bazaar*'s 1952 April issue. It was Audrey's first appearance inside the brilliant pages of the highly regarded fashion magazine. These series of events began a lasting relationship between Audrey Hepburn, Richard Avedon, and *Harper's Bazaar*.

Audrey would model before Avedon's cameras countless times over the years; she made history when she was the first movie star featured on the cover of *Harper's Bazaar* magazine in April 1956. On the vibrant cover, shot in Paris, Avedon took an artistic approach with his model. Only showing her face, Audrey is fully wrapped in a colorful floral-print scarf. Placed on top, she balances a wide-brimmed straw hat that dramatically frames her exquisitely painted face. In July of 1956, Audrey and Avedon worked together on Paramount's movie musical *Funny Face*. The lead male character, Dick

Avery (played by Fred Astaire), was loosely based on Avedon's career at *Harper's Bazaar*. His official screen credit in the film was "special visual consultant" but Avedon immersed himself well beyond his job title. He designed the opening credits for *Funny Face* and taught Astaire how to professionally hold a camera. He traveled to Paris with the crew to help set up shots and lend his expertise however possible. Even Audrey's character, Jo, was a nod to Avedon's first wife, the fashion model, Doe Avedon.

Richard Avedon began his career at *Harper's Bazaar* in 1944 at just twenty-one years old. He worked under the supervision of art director Alexey Brodovitch, who was also portrayed in *Funny Face* as *Quality* magazine's art director, Dovitch. It was Brodovitch who gave the young hopeful his first break after seeing a portrait he had photographed of two merchant marines while serving as a photographer's mate second class in the US Merchant Marine. He would praise Avedon's work, "It has surprise, shock, originality. His work arrests the eye and he has the sharpest eyes I know. He's like a stage director. He's not a push-button photographer as so many are."[62]

Avedon quickly rose through the ranks at *Harper's Bazaar* with the help of fashion photographer Lillian Bassman (with whom he worked at *Junior Bazaar*) and soon earned the position of chief photographer. "At the precise point when fashion photography had achieved absolute technical perfection, when fashion models looked like awesome chunks of ice awash in artificial light, Dick Avedon breezed into the art department of *Harper's Bazaar*,"[63] reported *New York Times* journalist Phyllis Lee in 1957. Only one other person at *Harper's Bazaar* could rival his spontaneity and use of movement, and that was the larger-than-life fashion editor Diana Vreeland. The two worked in tandem at *Harper's Bazaar*, combining their unparalleled skills to generate imaginative and avant-garde fashion spreads that showcased the most in-demand models in precarious situations. Naturally, it only made sense that in 1959 Richard Avedon would envision a cinematic fashion layout for *Harper's Bazaar* featuring none other than Audrey Hepburn.

The photo shoot was entitled "Paris Pursuit" and was slated for *Harper's Bazaar*'s upcoming September issue. Avedon visualized a fashion editorial that read like a screenplay. The "movie" would star Audrey Hepburn as Jemima Jones, a chic traveling actress, and Mel Ferrer as Dallas O'Hara, Esq., a traveling millionaire. To round out the cast, Avedon solicited the help of Hollywood heavy hitters like actor Buster Keaton, who played the role of "Big Thunderbrow, O'Hara's brave valet" as described in *Harper's Bazaar*, and actress Zsa Zsa Gabor, who was cast as "a Cocotte." Also asked to join the team was American humorist Art Buchwald as "The Man in the Hat at Maxim's" and Danish actress Annette Stroyberg as "a Seine-side Beatnique."[64] At the bottom of the credits page, listed beneath the cast's names, read "Directed by Richard Avedon."

OPPOSITE Richard Avedon and Audrey walking to their next shoot location. ABOVE TOP "Jemima Jones," holding her white cat, Simone, watches as "Dallas O'Hara" embraces another woman. ABOVE BOTTOM Audrey, wearing her white wool Chanel ensemble, with hairstylist Enrico Caruso.

The script was written by American author Truman Capote, who explicitly forbade his name from being included as retaliation after *Harper's Bazaar* canceled the publication of his book *Breakfast at Tiffany's*.

*Harper's Bazaar* set aside twenty pages and an undisclosed small fortune for this fantastical fashion treatment. Audrey Hepburn, along with a handful of models, including an Avedon favorite, China Machado, modeled the latest winter designs from Paris's leading fashion houses. Audrey wore a total of eighteen outfits. The designers chosen for the project were Dior, Cardin, Chanel, Grès, Laroche, Patou, Ricci, Lanvin, Heim, Dessès, Goma, Griffe, and Balmain. Noticeably missing from the list were Givenchy and Balenciaga. Customarily, both designers denied the press (which included fashion magazines) access to their collections until their clients had a chance to view them first. The daring, offbeat cover resembled a script's title page. Printed in bold white lettering inside solid black blocking on a stark white background, the cover reads, *HARPER'S BAZAAR* PRESENTS AUDREY HEPBURN, MEL FERRER, PARIS PURSUIT, A LOVE FARCE, FEATURING THE PARIS COLLECTIONS WITH BUSTER KEATON, DIRECTED BY RICHARD AVEDON PLUS THE AMERICAN FASHION OPENINGS.[65] The only hint of color was the word *BAZAAR* printed in a deep purple.

The plot, also known as the *pursuit*, tells the story of Jemima and Dallas and how they first meet at the Gare du Nord train station. Having just arrived in Paris, the two strangers are immediately lovestruck and engage in an awkward exchange. Jemima nervously begins to speak in French only to confuse the American cowboy. Discouraged, the two part ways and spend the rest of their time

ABOVE Avedon and an assistant helping Audrey with her outfit. Mel off to the side in his cowboy attire. OPPOSITE Audrey smoking between photo takes.

ABOVE TOP Avedon prepping to photograph Audrey and Mel on the Gare de Lyon bus. ABOVE BOTTOM Audrey and Mel photographed during a lull in shooting. OPPOSITE Avedon helping Audrey with her Dior dress at the Ritz Paris.

frantically searching for each other on the streets of Paris. Jemima confides in her white cat, Simone, "Oh, Simone, Simone, what a ring-a-ding divine guy! Why do I always have to be such a show-off and a fool? What a devil drives me! *Why did I pretend to be French!*"[66] To arrange a photo shoot at an empty Gare du Nord station, Avedon scheduled a 3:30 A.M. call time to avoid the morning crowds.

The fashion shoot was photographed in August in Paris and took five exhaustive days to complete. Avedon dragged Audrey and Mel around the city while the two actors reenacted their humorous scripted scenarios. *Harper's Bazaar*'s artistic director, Henry Wolf, was also in town, along for the ride. Wolf had recently been promoted to art director after Avedon's mentor, Brodovitch, left the magazine in 1958. He photographed Avedon and his cast as they set up their numerous shots all over Paris. His photos were laid out in *Elle* magazine's October 1959 issue. Also assisting Avedon was one of Mel Ferrer's sons from a previous marriage.

The first scene began Monday morning at 6:00 A.M. Audrey wore a voluminous stone-pale Lesur wool fleece coat by Grès with her hair pulled back in a high braided bun. Audrey had hand selected her wardrobe the previous month when she attended the Winter collections with Avedon during Paris fashion week. Jemima is photographed stepping off the back of the Gare de Lyon 63 bus. Dallas, wearing a cowboy hat and boots, watches as she kisses another man. In this sequence of events the two have been desperately looking for each other for days. They begin to see each other's face in everyone they meet as described in Capote's script, "It was Saturday. Then it was Sunday. The days went by as in a dream. Everywhere Jemima went, and everywhere she looked . . . and for Dallas it was the same."[67] In a photograph by Henry Wolf, Audrey poses on the back of the 63 bus with celebrity hairdresser Enrico Caruso, who tends to her tightly combed bun.

Caruso, a celebrity hairstylist with an impressive clientele including Marilyn Monroe and Grace Kelly, was hired by *Harper's Bazaar* to style Audrey's hair for the elaborate shoot.

The next morning, Tuesday, at 7:30 A.M. the crew arrived at a courtyard in Butte Montmartre. Avedon spent three hours staging his shot of Audrey, Mel, and Buster Keaton standing on the uneven cobbled streets. A clownish-looking Mel wearing false biceps is shown lifting papier-mâché barbells over his head as Audrey watches in amazement. The biceps and weights were purchased at a local flea market. Audrey wore a black ribbon lace evening dress by Michel Goma with a hooded jacket and layered skirt. At 5:30 P.M. they moved to the Impasse de l'Ancre near Pont de Neuilly (Neuilly bridge). Audrey, dressed in a Dior mustard tweed suit, looks over her shoulder to find Mel riding horseback along the cobblestone road.

Beginning at 9:00 A.M. on Wednesday, Audrey posed as twin college girls. With his ingenious use of the camera, Avedon displayed two images of Audrey side by side, creating the illusion of identical twins. Mel, dressed in his usual cowboy attire, is in the background trying to catch their attention. Enrico braided Audrey's hair into long pigtails, and to give her a collegiate look, she donned a pair of round spectacles purchased at the Kremlin-Bicêtre market. Dressed as one of the college girls, Audrey wears a scarlet wool jacket dress by Dior, and as her identical sister, a black-and-white wool jacket dress also by Dior.

On Thursday, the team was transported to two different locations starting at nine in the morning. The first was at a butcher's shop in Montparnasse. Audrey is dressed in a snow beige wool pinafore-style dress with two panels by Guy Laroche. The second setting was at *le commissariat de police*. Due to restrictions, the crew built a reproduction police station in studio and hired extras to play the officers. A naive Jemima, still in pursuit of her vanishing cowboy, employs the help of the police: "Well, no, he hasn't committed a crime. No, he's

not my husband. He isn't even a friend. Not really. Not exactly. I want to find him because . . . just because . . . because, *golly*, I guess he's the man I *love*."[68] Jemima, wearing a tan wool coat with blouson bodice by Cardin, wins the hearts of the sympathetic officers.

The final Paris scene took place on Friday at Maxim's, a popular restaurant at 3 rue Royale. The session began at 6:00 P.M. after the final dinner guests had left and lasted six long hours. Audrey was understandably nervous about slipping into her form-fitting Dior dress and avoided eating that day. The cast was treated to champagne and caviar while Audrey sipped from her glass of fruit juice. Audrey's hair was pulled tight into a conical-shape updo, a trendy new style in Paris fashions. Audrey wore Dior's white crystallized showstopper, the Armide dress, with a matching Dior *diamanté* dog collar. The Armide dress was a "puffed tunic silhouette [ . . .] beaded and spangled for evening in a shimmer of light."[69] The *shimmering* dress showed off Dior's suggestive new hemline that rose scantily above the knee every time Audrey made the slightest movement. Elizabeth Taylor also wore the Armide dress two months later at Leone's restaurant in New York. Leaning against the bar inside Maxim's, Audrey slyly looks over at Art Buchwald, who is wearing a cowboy hat and boots. Jemima says, "I hope you don't think I'm *that* kind of a girl or anything. The only reason I spoke to you, without really *knowing* you, is, well . . . there's *something* about you that reminds me of someone."[70]

In addition to Maxim's, the Ferrers and Avedon spent time shooting along the Seine, at the Hôtel Ritz, under the Eiffel Tower, and inside the Moulin Rouge, all leading up to the long-awaited moment where the two lovebirds finally reunite in the Swiss Italian Alps. Shown on the last two pages of the twenty-page *Harper's Bazaar* spread, Audrey and Mel are photographed zipping across a cable car high above the mountainside. In the photo to the right, Jemima is wearing a white satin long-sleeved wedding dress and Dallas is dressed in lederhosen. The sweethearts jauntily skip outside a Swiss chapel where they were newly married, a nice homage to Audrey and Mel's Swiss wedding in 1954. A happy ending!

The extensive shoot was a nice distraction for Audrey, who had suffered a miscarriage earlier that year. She was able to spend time in her favorite city observing the best of French fashions and playing dress-up at some of Paris's most mainstream attractions. The five-day shoot in Paris reunited Audrey with friends and allowed her to momentarily soothe her loss. For Avedon, the experience was a fun diversion from his typical day job. He excelled at the challenge of dual roles as photographer and creative director and couldn't have imagined a better model than Audrey. "Audrey Hepburn is a dream. She has great inventiveness and you get wonderful shots from her,"[71] Avedon said of his leading lady. Audrey was always at ease in the presence of Avedon; in front of his lens she felt protected. "I am and forever will be devastated by the gift of Audrey Hepburn before my camera," praised Avedon. "In a way that is unique in my experience as a photographer, I love her but I have always found her impossible to photograph. However you define the encounter of the sexes, she wins. I cannot lift her to greater heights. She is already there. I can only record, I cannot interpret her. There is no going further than who she is. She paralyzes me. She has achieved in herself her ultimate portrait."[72] *Harper's Bazaar*'s September issue flew off the shelves, solidifying what readers already knew: the alchemy between Audrey and Avedon was a visual masterpiece. ✳

---

OPPOSITE Enrico Caruso styling Audrey's conical-shape updo. She is wearing Dior's *shimmering* "Armide" dress.

# { 10 }

# Le Bal des Petits Lits Blancs

Nineteen sixty was an auspicious year for the thirty-one-year-old actress. On July 17, 1960, Audrey gave birth to her first child, Sean Hepburn Ferrer. After years of trying to conceive and enduring the heartbreak of multiple miscarriages, Audrey was over the moon about the arrival of her son. Her ultimate wish had been actualized: she was finally a mother. That same year in the fall Audrey flew to New York to begin production on her most memorable title, *Breakfast at Tiffany's*. Her performance as the free-spirited Holly Golightly was a commercial success and a fashion achievement for the reigning champions Hepburn and Givenchy. Audrey would spend the spring and summer months of 1961 in Los Angeles filming *The Children's Hour*, an emotionally grueling production with William Wyler, Shirley MacLaine, and James Garner. For now, Paris would have to wait. But in January of 1962, Audrey would visit Paris for a charity event in support of a cause close to her heart.

The Ferrers arrived in Paris the second week of January with a packed calendar brimming with social engagements. Audrey was in town to promote her latest film, *Breakfast at Tiffany's*, or as it was known in France, *Diamants sur Canapé*

OPPOSITE Audrey aboard the *France* cruise ship for Le Bal des Petits Lits Blancs. ABOVE Audrey with two French officers at the *Breakfast at Tiffany's* cocktail party at the Hôtel Plaza Athénée.

(*Diamonds on Canapé*). Audrey had turned down the flashy New York premiere of *Breakfast at Tiffany's* to stay home with her son in Switzerland. Sean, who was now seventeen months old, was her main concern. But seeing as Paris was a shorter commute from Switzerland than taking time off to fly to New York, Audrey accepted an invite to be a guest of honor at one of the biggest French charity events of the year, *Le Bal des Petits Lits Blancs* (The Ball of the Little White Beds). On January 12, Audrey and Mel visited the Hôpital Necker-Enfants Malades, a French children's hospital located on rue de Sèvres. Audrey spent time with the children and staff, who presented her with a bouquet of flowers as a token

of their appreciation. Her friend, photographer Jack Garofalo, was there to capture the tender moments between Audrey and the children.

Later that afternoon, Audrey attended a promotional cocktail party for *Breakfast at Tiffany's* hosted at the Hôtel Plaza Athénée located on avenue Montaigne. Audrey, wearing a brown sleeveless satin dress by Givenchy and a Van Cleef & Arpels brooch, was escorted by French police officers into the salon. To garner publicity for her new film, she was photographed holding a silver platter with individual caviar toasts decorated with diamonds from Van Cleef & Arpels worth, all together, $600,000. The police officers kept a close eye on Audrey as she presented the tray of diamonds to a room full of press.

The following day, on January 13, Audrey prepared for one of the most celebrated annual events in Paris, Le Bal des Petits Lits Blancs. The Ball of the Little White Beds began in 1917 to raise funds for the Saint-Louis hospital, which, at the time, was severely lacking in financial aid. The ball became an annual event and in 1962 was celebrating its twenty-ninth anniversary. Traditionally held at the L'Opera de Paris, this year's gala was given aboard the newly renovated cruise ship the *France*. On Saturday afternoon, an impressive sight of thirteen hundred people arrived at the ordinarily monotonous Gare Saint-Lazare railway station located in the Eighth Arrondissement of Paris. The lively flock of guests crowded the platform, each lugging suitcases for their oceanic voyage.

The women carefully protected their garment bags containing designer gowns by some of Paris's most established couturiers, including Pierre Balmain, Jean Dessès, Christian Dior, Jacques Esterel, and Jacques Heim. At 2:30 P.M., the animated crowd stepped aboard two special trains that transported them to Le Havre port, where they boarded the magnificent *France* at 5:30 P.M. They were then escorted to their individual cabins, giving them enough time to settle in before the evening's activities.

ABOVE TOP Audrey visiting with children at the Hôpital Necker-Enfants Malades. ABOVE BOTTOM Audrey and Mel posing for photographs in front of the *France*. OPPOSITE TOP Audrey surrounded by photographers in the dining room on board the *France*. OPPOSITE BOTTOM Audrey and Mel swarmed by party guests on the dance floor.

The liner had a crew of eleven hundred men who were at the guests' disposal for the next two days. Each patron paid the equivalent of $90 to attend the elegant affair, which raised a total of 45 million old francs for the *Union Nationale des Polios* (The National Union of Polio). The illustrious ocean liner, which never left the port, had two rooms designated for the evening's events. The first room was chaired by the Baroness de Seillière, the president of the works of the *Petits Lits Blancs*, and the second dining room was led by Commandant Georges Croisile, who was seated next to Ms. Hepburn and Mrs. Couve de Murville, the wife of the French minister of foreign affairs.

Among the prestigious guests were Princess Paola and Prince Albert of Liège and Princess Maria

ABOVE LEFT Audrey and Mel arriving at Le Bal des Petits Lits Blancs. ABOVE RIGHT Audrey and Mel dancing aboard the *France*.

Pia and Prince Alexander of Yugoslavia. Princess Paola, who was five months pregnant, wore a sleeveless dress of red-and-gold brocade. Her hair was sculpted sixteen inches high above her head and extravagantly displayed in the center was her gold filigree tiara. Princess Maria Pia wore a dress of brown tulle embroidered with crystal droplets. Audrey looked elegant in a sleeveless full-length ivory satin gown from Givenchy's 1961 Autumn Winter collection. The design, known as the Irene, was worn with a pearl gray bolero jacket trimmed with white mink and embroidered with pearls and crystals by the French embroidery brand Rébé.

Audrey debuted a new coiffure created by the acclaimed French hairstylist Alexandre de Paris. The "Little Cleopatra" was described as "a two-story hairdo" with "part of the hair drawn back following a receding line, while the other caresses the neck."[73] The "Cleo Look" was the new fad in fashion due to the popularity surrounding the upcoming Elizabeth Taylor movie, *Cleopatra*. Audrey's "Little Cleopatra" was slightly altered from the original design; in lieu of a half-pony, Audrey's hairdo was drawn up into a beehive and worn with blunt bangs covering her forehead. Placed on the side of her updo was a striking white bow that matched her snowy ensemble. After the successful launch aboard the *France*, the Little Cleopatra was later presented to the French fashion houses, including Givenchy, Laroche, Grès, Venet, and Hermès.

Before dinner began, Audrey was asked to host a lottery that comprised eight expensive prizes, including a Boucheron gold lighter and blue marble bath. Supper was served at approximately 8:30 P.M. On the menu was caviar, foie gras, sole, tournedos of beef, and a limitless supply of champagne, vodka, bordeaux, and cognac. After dinner, guests were shown to the auditorium aboard the *France*, where a special screening of *Breakfast at Tiffany's* was playing. Despite the grand scale of the room, which could seat 664 people, an additional four chairs had to be brought in for Prince and Princess Michel of Bourbon-Parma and the Ferrers. Many of the guests abandoned the movie prematurely to partake in the conga line forming in the hallways. Audrey and Mel were among those who snuck out early; they had already seen the film fifteen times. The couple made quite the impression in the grand salon. Curious onlookers swarmed the spirited couple and cheered in disbelief while Audrey and Mel wiggled their bodies to the newest dance craze, "The Twist." Everyone was surprised by the Ferrers' ability to let loose on the dance floor.

The gala turned into a lively evening; guests filled the three grand salons dancing the cha-cha, the farandole, the tango, and the twist. Scattered throughout the ship were six orchestras that performed into the wee hours of the night. At four o'clock in the morning, the partygoers were still going strong, at which point Audrey and Mel swapped partners and danced with the Prince and Princess of Liege. After the Ferrers withdrew for the evening, the party continued until seven in the morning. At 9:00 A.M. breakfast was served in the Tourists' dining room. Some people mustered up enough energy to make their way to the dining hall while others clung to their few extra minutes of sleep before departing that morning. The exhausted guests begrudgingly boarded the two trains back to Paris, where they reluctantly rejoined the real world.

Audrey had a good time aboard the luxury liner. More so, she was glad she could help raise money for victims of polio, a cause she had been involved with since the early 1950s. In New York in 1952, Audrey had walked in a charity fashion show for the March of Dimes, a foundation founded by president Franklin D. Roosevelt to help fight polio. When asked by a journalist how she felt about her time spent on the *France*, Audrey responded, "If my presence helps to do good, I am happy to be here."[74] Audrey and Mel were worn out from the last forty-eight hours. They returned home to their chalet in Bürgenstock to be with their son, Sean, whom they missed dearly; but it wouldn't be long before Audrey made her way back to Paris. In June, she would begin filming her next movie, *Paris When It Sizzles*. ✴

## { 11 }

# Paris When It Sizzles

I n April of 1962, Hubert visited Audrey at her home in Bürgenstock to discuss the wardrobe for her next film, *Paris When It Sizzles*. Production was slated to begin in June with Richard Quine at the helm for Paramount Studios. Audrey and Hubert were tasked with designing a modest wardrobe fit for Audrey's character, Gabrielle Simpson, a young secretary living in Paris. About to turn thirty-three, Audrey had topped the International Best-Dressed Hall of Fame List for the past six years and her costumes from *Breakfast at Tiffany's* had made a notable splash within the fashion industry. This time, the two carefully chose ensembles with pale colors and uncluttered lines.

Together, Audrey and Hubert chose six outfits. Four of the outfits included a pink sleeveless cocktail dress made of silk brocade, an ivory sleeveless day dress with a matching collarless jacket and blue leather belt, a delicate blue silk nightgown with a lace cape, and a renaissance gown with a conical headdress worn at a costume party at the Eiffel Tower. But Audrey's most noteworthy ensembles were an orange dress and a green suit. Her orange sleeveless dress of silk linen with a winged collar and matching ribbon around the waist was worn with a straw hat designed by French milliner Jean

Barthet and made specifically for the movie. Also sharing the bulk of screen time was a pistachio-colored wool suit with a collarless jacket and matching oversized buttons worn over a two-piece overblouse dress with a white sleeveless top and a pistachio green flared skirt with flap pockets at the hipline. As a finishing touch, Givenchy designed and added a white lacquered straw hat with a matching bow along the brim. After Audrey approved each design, Hubert returned to Paris to begin work.

Audrey arrived in Paris in early June with Mel, Sean, and her new Yorkshire terrier, Assam of Assam. In the past, Audrey had stayed at the Hôtel Raphaël, but now, as the mother of a two-year-old, hotel living no longer suited her needs. Instead, Audrey and Mel rented a seventeenth-century château in Yvelines,

OPPOSITE Audrey on the set of *Paris When It Sizzles*.
ABOVE Givenchy visiting Audrey and Mel (in costume) on the set of *Paris When It Sizzles*.

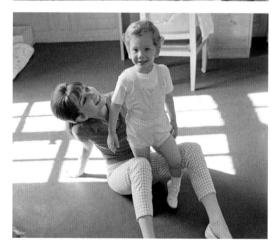

ABOVE TOP, MIDDLE, BOTTOM Audrey, Mel, and their son Sean photographed at Château de Crespières. OPPOSITE Audrey, Bill Holden, and director Richard Quine filming on "Richard Benson's terrace" during the production of *Paris When It Sizzles*.

France, for $3,000 a month. Château de Crespières, owned by Prince Michel de Bourbon-Parma, was located near Fontainebleau and was a convenient thirty-minute drive from the Studios de Boulogne. The private estate provided Sean with the comforts of home and allowed him ample space to run freely. The expansive grounds included a large lawn surrounded by sprawling trees and a pond. On the weekends, the Ferrers would spend time socializing outdoors on the estate.

Audrey was a protective mother and cultivated a home life separate from her career where she could shelter her son from the superficial demands of Hollywood. Her only desire was to provide Sean with a normal and structured life: "Even working before the cameras I want to be sure I am running my house properly: that my child is happy and calm and is having his meals on time; that Mel is being properly fed. I have to be sure that my home and family life run as smoothly as they can."[75] Audrey's greatest motive in life was security: a privilege she had been deprived of during her childhood years in war-torn Arnhem. She desperately wanted to present a stable family to her son to make up for the abandonment of her own father, a scarring memory that never healed. She kept Sean out of the limelight, away from photographers and the press. At Château de Crespières, Audrey could be a hands-on mother. She would spend her mornings at home with her son, and on the weekends the two would relax and play outside.

Like clockwork, each day Audrey rose at 7:00 A.M. and enjoyed an early breakfast with her son before privately running through her lines. Afterward, she would get dressed, typically choosing a classic shirt and slim trousers. At 9:00 A.M., a chauffeured car would arrive at the château and drive Audrey to the studio for makeup and wardrobe fittings at 11:00 A.M. Filming would officially commence at noon and finish around 8:00 P.M. Once again, a driver provided by Paramount would

collect Audrey from the studio and drive her home, where she would continue her preparations before retiring for bed simply to repeat it all the next day: "In the evening after dinner I only study for half an hour about the text, which I have to play in the studio the next day, and I go to bed before half past nine. The next morning I leave for the studio at nine o'clock, but luckily I have just a little more time to play with my son, Sean, because he is worth much, much more to me than any film role."[76]

Production began on June 18, 1962, at the Studios de Boulogne. *Paris When It Sizzles* was an American remake of the 1952 French film *La Fête à Henriette* (*Holiday for Henrietta*). Screenwriter George Axelrod, who had written the script for

*Breakfast at Tiffany's*, was asked to pen a modernized screenplay. Audrey was joined by her *Sabrina* costar William Holden in a zany romantic comedy about a Hollywood screenwriter, Richard Benson (William Holden), who has forty-eight hours to complete a screenplay for his boss, Alexander Meyerheim (Noël Coward). Benson hires Gabrielle Simpson, a young secretary, in a desperate attempt to type an entire screenplay before Bastille Day. *Paris When It Sizzles* was a frothy film with a thin plotline. Production was fraught with constant mishaps that impeded filming and the director's schedule. On the first day of filming a small fire broke out at the Studios de Boulogne after an arc light exploded on set. The fire department put out

the flames and the crew was able to resume shooting an hour later. The unlucky incident should have been a warning sign of things to come.

In August, Audrey's Swiss chalet was burglarized by two French students. The miscreants stole jewelry, clothes, silverware, a Picasso painting, and Audrey's Oscar statue for *Roman Holiday*. When they were questioned by authorities, the misguided robbers admitted they wanted badly to meet the Hollywood star and figured they'd get their chance in court. At the time, Audrey was filming at the Studios de Boulogne and Mel was in New York. A panic-stricken Audrey rushed home to Bürgenstock to assess the damage. On the way,

her chauffeur was involved in a small automobile accident but thankfully no one was hurt. Police were able to recover Audrey's Oscar, which they found abandoned in the woods near her home.

Unfortunately, there were further setbacks on the set of *Paris When It Sizzles*. Audrey and Bill Holden had not seen each other since *Sabrina*, where they had been briefly involved in an on-set affair. Audrey ended the relationship when she realized there was no future for her and Bill. Shortly after their breakup, she began dating her future husband, Mel Ferrer. Yet, despite their long absence, Bill was reportedly still in love with Audrey and his unrequited feelings coupled with his advanced alcoholism created a stressful environment. But Audrey was sympathetic toward Bill's condition and would invite him to join her family at Château de Crespières on the weekends. However, Bill would often show up drunk to the set, so in an

ABOVE LEFT Audrey in her pistachio-colored suit and white lacquered straw hat. ABOVE RIGHT Audrey wearing her sugary pink Givenchy dress. OPPOSITE Candid shot of Audrey on the set of *Paris When It Sizzles*.

attempt to help Bill and save production, Richard Quine sent Bill to a clinic to sober up. In July, newspapers reported that Bill was in the hospital with an eye infection, while rumors swirled that Bill had, in fact, undergone plastic surgery on his lower eyelids to appear more refreshed next to his youthful costar. With Bill in rehab, Quine was losing money and couldn't afford any further delays. Eager to carry on, he continued casting and hired Tony Curtis to join the struggling cast as a self-absorbed young actor. Filming resumed and Audrey, the ultimate professional, never complained.

. . . Well, that's not entirely true. In the past, Audrey had worked with cinematographer Franz Planer, but at the time of filming Planer was unavailable. As a result, production hired French cinematographer Claude Renoir. In France, Claude was considered French royalty. His father was actor Pierre Renoir, his uncle was director Jean Renoir, and his grandfather was the famous painter, Pierre-Auguste Renoir. Despite his reputation, his time on set was limited. After watching the daily rushes, Audrey expressed her disapproval. She was unhappy with her appearance and felt the lighting was unflattering. She asked that production remove Renoir and replace him with Charles Lang, the cinematographer from *Sabrina*. Quine complied and Renoir was fired. "Audrey's strong, very strong, and she was not happy with the way she looked,"[77] Quine recalled. Renoir's dismissal caused an uproar in France and nearly ended in a strike. But Renoir didn't leave on bad terms. He held a meeting and encouraged the crew to work accordingly with Lang. Thankfully, the uncomfortable situation was resolved and Audrey was satisfied with the final outcome.

At the time, *Paris When It Sizzles* was the biggest production shot at the Studios de Boulogne. Richard Quine had helicoptered over Paris in search of the perfect exterior shots for his $3.5 million movie. He settled on the forest glade of Les Yvelines, Place Dauphine, the Seine (past Île de

Cité), Bois de Boulogne, Champs-Elysées, avenue Matignon, the Grande Cascade, and the Eiffel Tower. The movie required four sets where they re-created some of Paris's most popular attractions. The crew spent $100,000 on a reproduction of Place Dauphine. Quine couldn't get permission to block off the real Place Dauphine for a consecutive two weeks, so Audrey filmed her scenes on a soundstage at the Studios de Boulogne. Another location built from scratch was Richard Benson's terrace apartment on avenue George V. The garden terrace was based on the actual terrace of actress Suzanne Flon (who asked to remain anonymous at the time). They re-created every piece down to the stones, the foliage, and the furniture selection. In some scenes, the cast and crew were allowed access to her actual terrace, which reportedly had the best views of the Eiffel Tower. The third stage constructed for the film was the first floor of the Eiffel Tower, where Audrey and Bill attend a costume ball. The final soundstage was used for multiple fantasy sequences within the movie. On this set, Audrey partook in her first on-screen bubble bath. She allowed only one still cameraman on set that day, her friend of many years, Bob Willoughby. To create the illusion of pink bubbles, a prop man stood off to the side spraying the bubbles pink for the color cameras. Newspapers reported that Paramount gifted Audrey the gold bathtub, which they speculated was sent to her home in Switzerland.

In August, Audrey filmed at the famous restaurant the Grande Cascade, located in the Bois de Boulogne. Audrey and Bill delighted in the nice weather at the restaurant's outdoor seating area. A sea of extras and colorful umbrellas surrounded the two while they acted out a scene from the character Richard Benson's screenplay. Filming outdoors presented its challenges. The director had less control of his surroundings and difficulty regulating sound and lighting. As a result, Audrey and Bill's dialogue at the Grande Cascade had to be dubbed due to noise disturbances. In the final scene, Audrey and Bill run hand in hand across the Trocadéro fountain. For a grand cinematic effect, the Trocadéro fountain was lit by a cascade of sparklers and a water show stretching as far as the eye can see. Audrey wore a pink silk sleeveless Givenchy dress with a matching sash tied at the waist. Alexandre de Paris was responsible for Audrey's elegant updo. He pulled her hair up into an oversize bun spun like a delectable French pastry with a pink bow placed plump in the center. The scene involved Audrey standing in the mist of the spraying fountains, so just to be safe, Richard Quine asked Givenchy to create four replicas of his sugary pink dress.

*Paris When It Sizzles* didn't wrap until November. Paramount was unimpressed with the original edit and required Audrey and Bill to report back to Paris in December to shoot additional scenes. Richard Quine was given an extra $100,000 to reedit the movie, but even so, the studio shelved *Paris When It Sizzles* for nearly two years, finally releasing it in April of 1964. During the final weeks of production, Audrey was juggling *Paris When It Sizzles* and wardrobe fittings for her next movie, *Charade*. After a tedious shoot, Audrey had a day to recuperate before reporting for duty on her next movie. Thankfully, she didn't have to go far. *Charade* was also filmed at the Studios de Boulogne. ✳

OPPOSITE Audrey and Bill photographed at the Grande Cascade restaurant.

# { 12 }
# Cocktails on the Seine

udrey had been working steadily since her late teens. Raised by her Dutch mother, she learned at an early age the importance of self-reliance and the value of hard work. As a consequence, she rarely allowed herself time off. If she wasn't filming, she was promoting a movie, posing for magazines, standing for fittings at Givenchy, traveling to movie locations with Mel, or at home raising Sean. However, during the production of *Paris When It Sizzles*, Audrey was hoping for a bit of amusement. In passing, she mentioned to a crew member her desire to take a boat trip on a bateau-mouche along the Seine River. She thought it would be a fun excursion and would give her the perfect opportunity to show William Holden all of Paris's charm. The request made its way to George Axelrod, the screenwriter and producer of *Paris When It Sizzles*, who found the idea beneficial for both parties. Here was an opening for him to grant Audrey her wish and garner publicity for the film. Although the movie had been shooting for less than a month, the production team wasted no time planning the outing.

The cruise was set for Thursday, July 4, 1962, aboard *La Galliote*. A hundred twenty-five guests from the international press were invited to join the two stars of *Paris When It Sizzles* for an evening of cocktails and music. Buzz about the junket

OPPOSITE AND ABOVE Audrey all smiles aboard *La Galliote*.

spread quickly; close to two hundred people arrived and actively made their way up the ramp and onto the boat. The bateau-mouche left the Pont de l'Alma at 6:00 P.M. and cruised along the Seine for two hours. They sailed past the Île Saint-Louis, Île de la Cité, Notre Dame, and the Louvre before circling back to their original port. Guests were treated to champagne and caviar and the smooth sounds of a five-piece cool jazz band. The boat was elegantly dressed with seasonal French flowers and a banner wrapped around the front railing with the words *PARIS WHEN IT SIZZLES* printed in large letters. Audrey, Bill Holden, Richard Quine, and George Axelrod greeted the guests as they boarded

the steamboat. Among the attendees was actor Jack Lemmon. In August, Audrey and Mel would celebrate Lemmon's upcoming nuptials to actress Felicia Farr at his engagement party in Paris. Also on board *La Galliote* were actors Yul Brynner, Marlene Dietrich, Nicole Maurey, Odile Versois, and Jean-Pierre Cassel, columnists Art Buchwald and John Crosby, and Martin Rackin, the head of Paramount Pictures. Everyone was enjoying themselves; according to the *Pittsburgh Post-Gazette*, "even a cynical, acid-penned French columnist remarked: 'The easiest-to-take cocktail party I ever attended.'"[78]

Reporters congregated around Audrey, who took everyone in stride. She was elegantly dressed in a two-toned Givenchy dress. The sleeveless top was of black satin with a bateau neckline accentuated by a thin black bow tied at the waist. The A-line skirt, made of white matte silk and gathered at the hips, matched her white Hermès evening gloves. On her feet, she wore a pair of René Mancini black satin kitten heels embellished with delicate satin bows at the point. Her hair was pulled up in a simple chignon, and her only accessories were a pair of oversized Oliver Goldsmith sunglasses (the same worn in *Breakfast at Tiffany's*) and a pair of Cartier pearl and diamond earrings (a gift from Mel).

The cruise docked at 8:00 P.M. The cheerful attendees made their way back onto land bubbling from the champagne and primed to write about the eventful evening. The *Paris When It Sizzles* team considered their shindig on the Seine a success. Audrey was thankful she could give her friend a unique tour of Paris. Admittedly, Bill understood Audrey's love for the effervescent city but still he remarked, "Nevertheless, I will return to Pasadena all the same. A hopeless old American."[79] ✳

ABOVE Audrey chatting with Jack Lemmon and Bill Holden aboard *La Galliote*. OPPOSITE Audrey and Bill sailing along the Seine for their *Paris When It Sizzles* press junket.

# 13

# The Longest Day Premiere

On the evening of September 25, 1962, Paris was in a flurry for the world premiere of *The Longest Day*. Darryl Zanuck's *The Longest Day* was an American epic war film about the D-day invasion in Normandy during World War II. It was promoted as the greatest war movie ever made—and the most expensive, with a budget of $10 million. Twentieth Century Fox spared no expense for the French premiere. They transformed the Palais de Chaillot by decorating the streets with paratroopers lined up between four Sherman tanks and six twenty-year-old 105 mm howitzers. The military equipment had been lent by a French war museum for the special occasion. Zanuck, one of the producers on the film and the new president of Twentieth Century Fox, cosponsored the world premiere with the four French veterans' organization.

The guest list was extensive and included ten generals and admirals, ten French cabinet ministers including Finance Minister Giscard d'Estaing; the ambassadors of England and the United States; multiple counts, countesses, barons, baronesses; international movie stars; and a smattering of Paris's most fashionable society. Invitations were also sent to Allied army commanders who campaigned in Europe after the landings in Normandy as well as statesmen including Winston Churchill and President Eisenhower (both of whom declined). A remarkable twenty-seven hundred people attended the premiere held at the Palais de Chaillot in the Trocadéro area in the Sixteenth Arrondissement of Paris. For the first time since the war, people were allowed to enter the hall through the Trocadéro Gardens.

OPPOSITE Audrey at the Palais de Chaillot for the premiere of *The Longest Day*. ABOVE Audrey and Mel arriving inside the Palais de Chaillot.

The palace gardens were beautifully lit by a fountain display that sprayed high above the courtyard.
Lining the gardens were French, American, English,
and Canadian army units in the Guard of Honor
while the knights of the Republican Guard rode in
on horseback gloriously sounding their trumpets.

Before the three-hour premiere began, respected
guests arrived at the Palais de Chaillot wearing their
most exquisite gowns and jewels. Among the invitees
were Audrey Hepburn and her husband, Mel Ferrer.
Mel, who played Major General Robert Haines in
*The Longest Day*, escorted his wife, who was in town
shooting *Paris When It Sizzles* at the Studios de
Boulogne. Audrey chose a more whimsical look for
the extravagant gala. She wore a custom-made dress
from Givenchy's 1962 Winter collection. The short-
sleeved beaded gown was a beautiful shade of pink
silk with a full-length skirt and a hemline that was
slightly shorter in the front. The intricate beadwork
consisted of rose montee crystals, pink bugle beads,
clear seed beads, and metallic thread embroidery
that dripped over the bodice and cascaded down the
length of the skirt. The dress sparkled from every
direction, matching the brilliance of the Eiffel Tower
that glimmered in the horizon. Audrey accessorized
the dress with a pair of diamond Cartier earrings
and white Hermès opera gloves. Her hairstyle was
created by Alexander de Paris and first worn during
a bubble bath scene in *Paris When It Sizzles*. Styled
high on her head, Audrey's hair was combed upward
into a tall chignon with blunt bangs. A separate section of her hair was wrapped around the bun and
flanked by two winged pieces that curled over her
ears. Placed in the back, under the fanciful updo, was
a single white satin bow. The hairstyle was a play-
ful departure for Audrey, who usually chose a more
understated look.

PAGE 102 Audrey with Baron and Baroness de Rothschild
watching the fireworks from inside the Palais de Chaillot.
PAGE 103 Fireworks erupting at the Eiffel Tower for *The
Longest Day* premiere. ABOVE Audrey and Mel enjoying
their champagne supper. OPPOSITE Édith Piaf giving a
memorable performance for all of Paris.

Other well-known names in attendance were director Otto Preminger, actress Catherine Deneuve, author Françoise Sagan and her husband, Bob Westhoff, German actor Curd Jürgens, French actor Jean-Louis Barrault, actor and singer Eddie Constantine, actress Irina Demink, and Audrey's very dear friend, actress Deborah Kerr. The United States ambassador to France, Lieutenant General James M. Gavin, portrayed by actor Robert Ryan in the movie, spent his farewell evening at the premiere before leaving his dignitary post as ambassador to France the next day.

The proceeds raised from ticket sales benefited the Veterans' Relief Fund and the fund to support war widows and orphans. Of the 2,700 guests, the 500 who paid the higher ticket price, equivalent to $70, were invited to a champagne supper arranged at the restaurant inside the Palais de Chaillot. Among the select group were Audrey and Mel, who enjoyed a catered dinner and a midnight concert given by France's most revered songstress, Édith Piaf. All of Paris remained awake to listen to the French singer belt from the first floor of the Eiffel Tower, 187 feet high above the ground.

Standing at only four feet ten inches, Édith Piaf sang before a dazzling fireworks display that blasted off in front of the Eiffel Tower. Everyone oohed and ahhed when a fiery eruption of the words *Le Jour le plus long* (the movie's title in French) pierced the midnight sky. Inside the restaurant, the Ferrers were seated between their close friends Baron Guy and Baroness Marie-Hélène de Rothschild. The foursome's table was in view of the Jardins du Trocadéro, giving them an uninterrupted view of the blazing rockets bursting overhead.

From half a mile away, television cameras broadcasted Ms. Piaf's performance onto a large screen in the main hall of the Palais de Chaillot. Thousands of Parisians stayed up past their bedtime to gather in the streets hoping to catch a glimpse of Piaf's pyrotechnic performance. Édith's

voice reverberated throughout the city. One French newspaper described the performance as "the two most celebrated Parisians, the longest and the shortest—the Eiffel Tower and Édith Piaf."[80]

As the last firework flickered in the night's sky, all of Paris, still with stars in their eyes, journeyed home. The premiere left a lasting impression on those who were lucky enough to partake in the evening's festivities. Like Cinderella, Audrey collected her glass slipper and returned home after a memorable night. Watching Édith Piaf bewitch all of Paris induced a feeling of nostalgia. Nearly a decade earlier Audrey had serenaded Humphrey Bogart in the movie *Sabrina*—during a romantic car ride, Sabrina purrs the lyrics "*Il me dit des mots d'amour, des mots de tous les jours, et ça me fait quelque chose*" like a haunting lullaby. Audrey would sleep away the excitement and resume work at the Studios de Boulogne as production began to wind down on *Paris When It Sizzles*. However, for one singular night, Paris lived up to its name, the City of Lights. ✶

# 14

# Charade

After the completion of *Paris When It Sizzles* in the fall of 1962, Audrey had planned to take a much-needed break. Her name was already attached to the upcoming Hollywood adaptation of *My Fair Lady*, scheduled to begin production in the summer of 1963. She was anticipating a nice vacation between films when a last-minute script fell into her lap. Stanley Donen had acquired the rights to a novel published in *Redbook* magazine; it was called "The Unsuspecting Wife" by Peter Stone. Donen knew that this was the perfect vehicle for his dream casting and asked Stone to tailor the script for his two choice leads: Audrey Hepburn and Cary Grant. Hollywood had been trying to partner Audrey and Cary on-screen since *Roman Holiday* and Audrey reveled at the opportunity to finally work with the eminent actor whom she had admired from afar. In a moment of spontaneity, Audrey agreed to *Charade* and extended her stay at Château de Crespières through the new year. "It was one of those quick and effective deals when everything seems to fall into place," recalled Audrey's agent Henry Rogers. "[Audrey and Cary] fit each other to a tee, both sporting the same air of vivacious mischief, yet they had never worked together as a team."[81]

*Charade* is the story of a recently widowed Regina Lampert, who finds herself in the throes of espionage and deception. The movie begins with Regina vacationing at a ski resort in Megève, France, when she meets an unassuming, handsome stranger named Peter Joshua (Cary Grant). The two engage in a witty repartee with Peter asking, "We don't know each other, do we?" and Regina answering, "I'm afraid I already know a great many people. Until one of them dies I couldn't possibly meet anyone else." Famous last words from our leading lady. Upon her return to Paris she is horrified to discover that her apartment has been emptied and all that remains are bare walls, scuffed floors, and a deadpan police inspector. The inspector informs Regina that her husband, Charles Lampert, has been murdered on a train departing Paris. The plot unfolds when three suspicious characters (James Coburn, George Kennedy, and Ned Glass) show up looking for a stolen fortune that was once connected to Charles. Thrown into the mix is a CIA operative (Walter Matthau), who is also in search of the missing money and concealing a few secrets of his own. The story surrounding her husband's death becomes entangled in doubt and misdirection and Regina soon finds herself in danger. Peter Stone spins a suspenseful web mired in humor and mystery all leading to a thrilling chase scene between Audrey Hepburn, Cary Grant, and Walter Matthau at the Jardin du Palais Royal. *Charade* is often referred to as "the best Alfred Hitchcock movie Hitchcock never made,"[82] based on the

OPPOSITE Audrey, photographed by Hamilton Millard, on the set of *Charade*.

movie review by David Bianculli. Like Hitchcock, Donen seamlessly intertwines the artful twists and turns with the romantic subplot between Regina and Peter, keeping the audience on their toes until the very end.

Considering there were only days between the time *Paris When It Sizzles* wrapped and *Charade* began filming, Audrey and Hubert didn't have a moment to spare when selecting the wardrobe. The seasoned duo began picking designs suitable for a wealthy American widow living in Paris. Together,

they decided on nineteen costumes. Their partnership was a well-oiled machine as described by Audrey: "When Givenchy and I select styles for a motion picture, we pay little attention to what is the current vogue. First we decide what would be appropriate to the character I enact. Then we decide what is appropriate for me. The current hemline, the favored-at-the-moment silhouette are ignored. For my personal use away from the cameras, I insist on clothes that are 'me.' I believe this to be an excellent blueprint for any girl who wishes to appear to advantage."[83]

Audrey favored clean lines, solid colors, and minimal accessories. For *Charade*, they decided on an assortment of coats, dresses, suits, and hats that were indicative of Hubert's new Winter collection. She chose two wool crepe dresses with a funnel

ABOVE Audrey wearing her Givenchy two-piece black crepe dress on the set of *Charade*. OPPOSITE TOP Audrey wearing her red coat inside Bartholomew's office. OPPOSITE BOTTOM Audrey wrapped in a red blanket to keep warm during filming.

neckline and short raglan sleeves with a black suede belt buckled at the waist, one in beige and one in yellow. She also selected a lightly fitted, single-breasted beige wool coat with collar à revers and a matching felt pillbox hat. Regina wore this outfit when she returned to Paris to find her apartment gutted. Audrey also specifically selected this coat for her personal wardrobe, saying, "It is classic, and it will be excellent for travel, especially in the spring and summer."[84]

Always striking in red, Regina arrives at Hamilton Bartholomew's office in a red raglan-sleeve wool coat with a funnel collar paired with a leopard-print dome hat. Audrey kept this coat until it was no longer wearable: "I had a red coat—the one in *Charade*—by Hubert, of course. I wore it until the threads began to separate and it was all shiny on the edges."[85] In a scene where Regina and Peter play a silly game involving an orange, Audrey wears a beautiful two-piece black crepe dress with jet beading trim and matching jacket. Another piece she selected for her own closet was a navy blue wool suit she wore in the final scene when she meets with Cary Grant at the American Embassy. "I just wore it for an instant," Audrey shared with Bernadine Morris of the *New York Times*. "Most clothes that you wear in a film get so burned out by the lights, the material looks tired and you become bored with them, you wear them so much."[86] Audrey balanced her outfits with a pair of white kid gloves, pearl earrings, and a variety of hats specially designed by Hubert, noting, "I think the most important part of a look is line, and the line of a dress or coat often looks incomplete without a hat—it is as if the shade were missing from the lamp."[87]

By 1962, Audrey's hair was mid-back length and often pulled up in a neat chignon. With Donen's authorization, she was given permission to choose her character's hairstyle. Though she had worked with Grazia de Rossi in the past, she was otherwise occupied, and Audrey needed someone to

quickly fill Grazia's shoes. Audrey made an unexpected decision and hired a French hairdresser by the name of Madame La Lorette to style her hair for *Charade*. Mel introduced Audrey to Madame La Lorette after having worked with her on the set of *L'homme à Femmes*. "I simply apply a 'postiche,' a kind of rolled up braid, and I give a sideways motion to the hair on her neck. This hairstyle, which is seen throughout the film, was created by the actress herself; she submitted it to the director and they went along with it," Madame La Lorette described in an interview from 1962. "The problem lies in doing it, again and again every morning, strictly identical to the previous one."[88] Re-creating Audrey's hairstyle wasn't a simple task. For continuity purposes, her chignon had to be perfectly intact and identical in every scene. Since it was "mandatory that not a single lock of hair appear out of place,"[89] Madame La Lorette took photographs of Audrey's hairstyle to make sure it was always camera ready.

For makeup, Audrey hired her go-to makeup artist, Alberto de Rossi. "Alberto is one of the men in my life. He is one of the dots in my movie contract—I am not filming without him. I even brought poor Alberto to the Congo," Audrey told reporter Mikael Katz on the set of *Charade*.[90]

Production began in late October of 1962. Donen wanted to highlight his three stars: Audrey Hepburn, Cary Grant, and the heart of the film, Paris. He began scouting locations in October but was met with opposition, in particular by the French authorities. They denied his first seven requests. The French police worried that filming would cause an increase in traffic in an already overcrowded city. All was not lost; Donen was able to establish filming locations at some of Paris's most enticing spots including Notre Dame, Jardins

des Champs-Elysées, Jardin du Palais Royal, and the Comédie-Française. The interior shots were filmed at Audrey's old stomping grounds, the Studios de Boulogne. "You may call me a permanent fixture at the Studios de Boulogne," Audrey said in jest. "I am one of those who can say 'remember when?'"[91]

*Charade* was Audrey's third movie filmed at the Paris studio. Marguerite Brachet, a wardrobe stylist at the Studios de Boulogne, fondly said, "Madame Hepburn was a delightful child, then, and is one now."[92] Yet the studio had changed since Audrey filmed *Love in the Afternoon*, and the adjoining black lot had been replaced with apartment buildings. Granted, some things remained the same; for example, the furniture used in *Charade* was said to be the same furniture used in *Love in the Afternoon*. And when Audrey was filming *Paris When It Sizzles*, she asked for dressing room 55. Room 55 was a significant number in Audrey's life; it was the same dressing room number she had occupied while filming *Breakfast at Tiffany's* in New York and *Roman Holiday* in Rome. At the time it was unavailable, but due to her well-established relationship with the studio, they made the necessary arrangements and were able to fulfill her request. Surprisingly, this was Cary Grant's first time filming in Paris. The closest he had come was at the Rex Ingram studio on the Riviera in 1954 when he filmed *To Catch a Thief*.

Paris was experiencing its coldest winter in decades. Audrey's Givenchy wardrobe may have looked effortlessly chic on camera, but it did little to stave off the bitter days. She recalled, "The nights Cary and I were running in his chase at the Palais Royal (really the Comédie-Française), tears were streaming down my face it was so cold. The streets weren't wet from rain; they were slick with ice. We laughed on the outdoor sets all the time; we laughed sometimes just to try to stay warm."[93] The piercing temperatures also made for some hazardous conditions as described by Stanley Donen: "Cary still has bruises on his legs from slipping. On

those running scenes with Audrey, we would do the same scene ten times. I was afraid my actors would drop from exhaustion."[94] Audrey and Cary did their best to keep warm while filming outdoors. Cary wore long underwear under his suit and Audrey bundled up in between shots. One of the coldest scenes to shoot was the romantic dinner cruise on the bateau-mouche. The Seine was covered in ice blocks and the crew used a machine to keep the boat from freezing. "We had to wear extra makeup because we continually turned blue,"[95] Audrey remarked. It was 30 degrees when Audrey and Cary walked along the left bank enjoying an ice cream cone. After six takes Audrey was practically ice herself. Shivering from the cold, she teased, "Now for a hot cup of coffee—and I hope my goose bumps won't register in Technicolor."[96]

Audrey and Cary adored working with each other. Both had earned sterling reputations in the industry for their unmatched professionalism. Audrey couldn't help but gush about her costar, "Cary is the most wonderful, most professional, most thorough and exacting actor I've had the pleasure of working with."[97] Prior to *Charade*, Cary had turned down the lead roles in *Roman Holiday*, *Sabrina*, and *Love in the Afternoon*; but after ten years of desperately trying to unite the two, Audrey and Cary proved to be Hollywood perfection. Cary had nothing but reverence for his costar: "In spite of her fragile appearance, she has great vitality. She's like steel. She bends but never breaks. We worked well together. She's considerate, always up on her lines, doesn't fuss and she seems to realize that other people on the set have their troubles,

TOP Audrey and Cary in front of "Hotel Saint Jacques" on 24 rue Censier. BOTTOM Audrey and Cary filming a scene on the left bank in front of Notre-Dame Cathedral. OPPOSITE Audrey, Mel, and Cary at the Comédie-Française for the 75th anniversary of the *New York Herald Tribune*'s European edition.

too."[98] Audrey was the first to wrap on the set of *Charade* in January and the entire crew felt her absence. Cary recounted, "She mothered the entire company. Day she left we were bereft. We had to stick around and do our fight scenes without her, and we were all furious."[99]

Audrey and Cary were introduced in Paris before production began, but it wasn't the meet-cute she had imagined. Audrey's nerves got the better of her, which resulted in a memorable first impression that eventually made its way into the picture. Audrey recalled, "Cary and I had never met before we did *Charade*, so there we all were in Paris, about to have dinner at some terribly smart bistro. As it was early spring, Cary, who always dressed impeccably, was wearing an exquisite light-tan suit. I know I was thrilled to meet him, and I must have been terribly excited, because not ten seconds after we started chatting I made some gesture with my hand and managed to knock an entire bottle of red wine all over poor Cary and his beautiful suit. He remained cool. I, on the other hand, was horrified. Here we'd only just been introduced!"[100] Audrey was mortified by her regrettable blunder and profusely apologized while Stanley watched the entire scenario play out before his eyes. Cary, who was every bit the gentleman off-screen as he was on, removed his wine-soaked jacket and, as Audrey put it, "pretended, very convincingly, that the stain would simply go away."[101]

With his keen directorial eye, Donen recognized the levity in the embarrassing encounter. It was so perfectly choreographed, it was as if it had been lifted off the page. He reworked the mishap into the script but swapped out wine for an ice cream cone. In the scene, Regina and Peter (now going by the alias Alex) are walking along the Seine near Notre Dame when Regina, holding her ice cream cone, turns toward Peter and asks, "This is good. Want some?" She clumsily knocks her ice cream on to the lapel of his suit. "No, thanks," Peter says. He grabs

the cone and throws it into the river, shrewdly saying, "And I guess you don't, do you?"

On November 29, while *Charade* was still in production, Audrey, Mel, Cary, and actress Jean Seberg attended a lavish evening at the Comédie-Française in honor of the seventy-fifth anniversary of the *New York Herald Tribune*'s European edition. Twelve hundred guests, including the minister of information, fifteen ambassadors, and famous Parisian personalities, filed into the Paris theatre located at 2 rue de Richelieu on the Place André Malraux. The attendees were treated to the first two acts of the comédie-ballet *Le Bourgeois Gentilhomme*. Following the performance, the guests were escorted by the stage actors, still in their coats and powdered wigs, to an impressive spread of buffets and drinks. Audrey was the epitome of chic in a long black silk satin shantung evening gown by Givenchy with detachable

cape and puffed capped sleeves. Her hair was swept up into a high bun pinned with a hair ornament made of black silk flowers and leaves. Cary and Mel looked equally dapper in their black tuxedos.

The following month, shortly before Christmas, photographer Hamilton Millard was invited by Audrey to photograph the Ferrers spending a day Christmas shopping in Paris. Audrey and Hamilton had first met on the set of *The Nun's Story* and remained in touch over the years, working together on the set of *Paris When It Sizzles* and reuniting again for *Charade*. Sean, who was now two years old, was proving to be tall like his father. Audrey saw how quickly Sean was growing and wanted

ABOVE AND OPPOSITE Audrey, Mel, and Sean (and their Yorkshire terrier Assam) Christmas shopping in Paris.

new photos of the family for their yearly Christmas cards. She thought a candid day of shopping would be a fun excursion for the family. The Ferrers, along with Sean's nanny, Gina; their Yorkshire terrier, Assam; and Hamilton, strolled through the festively lit Parisian streets. All together, they entered a department store where Sean was immediately taken by the toy store and all its delights. Not long after their outing, Millard mailed the final photos to Audrey. After careful examination, she chose a photo of her, Mel, Sean, and Assam smiling at the camera as they rode an escalator inside a department store. In Audrey's penmanship, the card read MERRY CHRISTMAS AND ALL OUR LOVE. Initially, the photos were meant for Audrey's private use, but to Millard's surprise, Audrey rang him up and gave him permission to sell the photos to the magazines of his choosing. The press had been unkind to the Ferrers' marriage and perhaps Audrey thought the photos would silence the unrelenting divorce rumors.

On New Year's Eve, Audrey and Mel hosted a formal gathering at their rented château in Yvelines, France. The Ferrers planned for an intimate evening among friends. They invited Cary Grant and his girlfriend, actress Dyan Cannon; Mr. and Mrs. Stanley Donen; and Mr. and Mrs. Peter Stone. Usually, Audrey preferred a more casual atmosphere, but on this occasion, she wanted to create a fancy dining experience for her guests. She hired staff wearing white gloves to serve the dinner. Writer Peter Stone remembered the celebratory dinner to be "as glamorous an evening as one can imagine, but it was truly boring."[102] According to Stone, everyone was in low spirits, including Audrey and Mel, who "were arguing a bit." Nonetheless, the food made a memorable impression as Stone recalled, "New Year's Eve, we had an enormously elegant affair at Mel and Audrey's where she served these gigantic Idaho baked potatoes and Cary brought a huge tin of caviar, and we spooned the caviar and sour cream

into the potatoes."[103] The potatoes with caviar were such a hit that they became an annual New Year's Eve tradition in the Hepburn household, sometimes replacing caviar for salmon. Shortly after filming concluded, Cary sent Audrey a gift of matching luggage and declared, "All I want next Christmas is another picture with Audrey."[104]

*Charade* wrapped in January 1963. The movie would premiere at the end of the year to rave reviews. It would become Stanley Donen's most successful movie and secure Audrey's ranking as one of Hollywood's most sought after actresses. Before returning home to Switzerland, Audrey attended a press conference for *Charade* at the Hôtel Ritz in February. On April 7, 1963, the day before the 35th Academy Awards was held at the Santa Monica Civic Auditorium, Audrey pre-

recorded a segment in Paris presenting the Best Costume award. She appeared in the same glittering pink Givenchy evening gown she had worn to *The Longest Day* premiere back in September. Later that month she flew to Madrid to visit Mel while he was filming *Fall of the Roman Empire*. Audrey kept busy in her spare time before reporting to Los Angeles in June for her next film for Warner Brothers. But before then, in March 1963, Audrey would make an appearance at Givenchy's salon for a *Vogue* photo shoot called "The Givenchy Idea." ✴

# { 15 }
# Vogue—The Givenchy Idea

In the last twelve years, Audrey had earned the title of *Vogue* darling since her magazine debut in November 1951. Her cosmopolitan taste and loyal friendship with Givenchy confirmed her as an international style icon, with her influence often seen on the Paris runways and in New York boutiques. Audrey's cultural impact as a trendsetter secured her standing on the Best Dressed lists and kept her in constant rotation on the glossy pages of fashion magazines. As such, it only seemed fitting that *Vogue* invited Audrey to unveil the newest designs by Givenchy in an unprecedented ten-page celebrity fashion spread called "The Givenchy Idea," published on April 15, 1963.

In March of 1962, after twenty-five years with *Harper's Bazaar*, Diana Vreeland was announced as the new editor in chief at *Vogue*. Diana and Audrey had a long-standing friendship rooted in mutual admiration and a deep appreciation of beauty. Audrey had worked with Diana on numerous occasions during her time at *Harper's Bazaar*, gracing multiple covers and appearing in Richard Avedon's brainchild, "Paris Pursuit," for their September 1959 issue. Vreeland's career was driven by her imagination; she naturally intuited trends six months before they happened and over time transitioned *Harper's Bazaar* and *Vogue* from fashion templates to fashion bibles. Grace Mirabella, Diana's right-hand woman and future *Vogue* editor in chief, explained it best, "Vreeland had learned in her early childhood days that the mundane realities of everyday life were not interesting—at least not to her. You had to exaggerate and embellish the world, make it more vibrant and beautiful."[105]

Vreeland's brilliance had been affectionately satirized in the 1957 film *Funny Face* starring Audrey Hepburn and Fred Astaire. Kay Thompson portrayed a sensationalized version of Vreeland as *Quality* magazine's editor in chief, Maggie Prescott. The "Think Pink" musical number was inspired by Diana Vreeland's ingenuity and innovative use of colors in her famous fashion editorials. Even the word *pizzazz* is said to have come directly from Diana Vreeland. As explained in Stanley Donen's biography *Dancing on the Ceiling: Stanley Donen and His Movies* by Stephen Silverman, the playwright Leonard Gershe was told by one of Diana's editors, D. D. Dixon, that Diana would often use the term "bizzazz." Gershe loved the nonsensical word so much that he included it in the final screenplay; however, somewhere along the way, the word was misinterpreted as "pizzazz." No matter, no one noticed the oversight and even Vreeland agreed that *pizzazz* was better than the original.

Diana held Audrey in high regard. She was inspired by her natural sophistication and gentle disposition. She even kept a photo of Audrey from

the set of *Paris When It Sizzles* pinned on the wall at her *Vogue* office. "I send you much much love and don't forget you are one of my favorite people,"[106] she wrote to Audrey in 1984. It was well known that Diana disliked the word *elegance*. She felt it was contrived and overused; yet, when she was asked to give her personal definition, she said, "It's a thing of bone and spirit. It exists in animals like the gazelle. Audrey Hepburn and a few people have

it."[107] Diana's reverence for Audrey made her the perfect choice to showcase Hubert's recent collection for *Vogue*'s upcoming feature.

On a quiet morning in March of 1963, a decade after Audrey and Hubert were introduced, a bright-eyed Audrey arrived promptly at 3 avenue George V for a full day of fashion fittings. Accompanied by her husband, Mel Ferrer, Audrey made her way to the salon inside the atelier where they were embraced by Givenchy's staff and the pleasant vibrations of French bossa nova music emanating from a record player. *Vogue* spent the entire day with Audrey from nine in the morning until midnight as she tried on various pieces from Givenchy's haute couture Spring collection. *Vogue* recorded Audrey's impression of each piece, "I want to make some dream-choices for *Vogue*, as if I was in a candy store."[108] They patiently sat with her as Roger Thiery, from Alexandre de Paris's salon, and his team of assistants styled Audrey's hair for each ensemble. Thiery created Audrey's imaginative updos (consisting of loops, twists, and knots) by using a combination of Audrey's own hair and fake lacquered hairpieces stacked on a cone-shaped postiche propped on top of her head and held together with bone hairpins. Showing no signs of fatigue, Audrey modeled each dress before Bert Stern's camera.

Stern had first worked with *Vogue* in the fall of 1960, photographing Deborah Dixon for the cover of their November 15 issue. This was Audrey's first time working with the young American fashion photographer. Stern instinctively knew how to capture Audrey's elongated and exaggerated features. His minimalist style effortlessly complemented Givenchy's polished designs and Audrey's feminine aura. Right away, Audrey was charmed by a pink fairy-esque gown: "The gossamer quality, the whole idea of it fascinated me; it's a dress that has to be worn."[109] *Vogue* described the dress as "a cocoon of romancey pink tulle with an inner layer of embroidery—mother of pearl, paillettes, sequins, glittery pink and silver thread—and yards of white tulle stole."[110] A color photo of Audrey modeling this cocoon-inspired dress was used for the cover of *Vogue Paris*'s May 1963 issue. Hubert de Givenchy also chose an image of Audrey in his pink creation for the promotion of his fragrance *L'Interdit*.

L'Interdit, French for "forbidden," was designed exclusively for Audrey in 1957, the same year Hubert established his own perfume label, *Parfums Givenchy*.

Hubert envisioned a perfume that would complement the clothes he designed for Audrey. In 1958, the house of Givenchy launched two new fragrances, *Le De* and, with Audrey's approval, *L'Interdit*. (This was the first time L'Interdit was made accessible to the public.) Le De, "De" the particle taken from Hubert's name, was advertised as a floral scent for daytime while L'Interdit was described as a "provocative fragrance for after dark wear."[111]

"That was the time I launched two perfumes," Givenchy reminisced. "I thought that if one didn't sell then the other would sell better! My meeting with Audrey at that time was crucial. I thought her image harmonized with the very essence of that fragrance. To associate the image of an actress with a perfume was an innovative step."[112] The two perfumes were

OPPOSITE Audrey wearing a yellow silk evening dress made of gauzy dotted shantung. ABOVE Audrey and Mel on the cover of Paris *Vogue* May 1963.

Once she was the only woman in the world allowed to wear this perfume. L'Interdit. Created by Givenchy for Audrey Hepburn.

available for purchase first in Europe in 1958 and then in the States in mid-April of 1960, christening L'Interdit as the first official celebrity fragrance. The perfume also made an unlikely appearance in the opening credits of *Paris When It Sizzles* under "Miss Hepburn's Wardrobe and Perfume—Hubert de Givenchy." Despite the impossibility of enjoying the sweet-smelling aroma through the screen, L'Interdit was still given the movie star treatment.

In 1957, Hubert commissioned French perfumer Francis Fabron to create the aromatic bouquet of scents for L'Interdit. The top notes were a delicate blend of aldehydes and bergamot complemented by a warm burst of strawberry and peach that softly lingered on the skin. The middle notes were a floral melody of iris, narcissus, rose, and ylang-ylang, with a musky, sexy undertone of sandalwood, amber, and vetiver for the base notes. L'Interdit was Audrey's signature scent and quickly became a favorite among

Givenchy's clients. Never motivated by money, Audrey refused to accept any profits from the perfume sales and considered it her gift to Hubert. An ad for L'Interdit featuring Audrey's image premiered inside the pages of *Vogue Paris* in May 1963 and *American Vogue* in June of 1963. In a full-page color advertisement, an ethereal Audrey gazes off beyond the camera's lens. Her swanlike neck was swathed in a shroud of white tulle, expressly drawing focus to her beautifully made-up face. The caption under the photo read, "Once she was the only woman in the world allowed to wear this perfume."[113]

"The Givenchy Idea" was featured in *Vogue*'s April 15, 1963, edition. Audrey chose each item highlighted in the attention-grabbing fashion editorial. It was her first time participating in a fashion spread of this measure for *Vogue* magazine but far from her last. Eight months later, Audrey appeared again in *Vogue* for their December issue modeling Cecil Beaton's costumes for *My Fair Lady*. The following year, she was chosen for the cover of *Vogue*'s November 1 issue in which she was featured in another ten-page fashion editorial showcasing her favorite designs from Givenchy's Winter collection. Audrey developed an enduring relationship with the prominent fashion magazine. She was consistently featured in fashion spreads and graced the covers of *Vogue*, *Vogue Paris*, and *British Vogue* a total of four times throughout her illustrious career. In September of 1971, Diana Vreeland wrote to Audrey to inform the then semiretired actress that her April 1 cover issue was the highest-rated printing since the magazine's inception in 1880. In the letter she tenderly writes, "You are always the most appealing creature there ever was and remain persistently the elegant, fragile child-woman."[114] Audrey and Diana remained close friends until the editor's death in 1989. ✳

ABOVE Givenchy's L'Interdit ad featuring Audrey.
OPPOSITE Audrey wearing a china-blue cloqué silk déshabillé.

J ust beyond the pale-buff façade of the house of Givenchy, three broad steps lead to the level of his gay little boutique; more stairs wind gently upward to the salon. Booming from the above at the press opening this spring, a plummy British voice asked tout Paris: "Isn't she a darling?" The sound led straight to Audrey Hepburn, smiling and ethereal, on the arm of her husband Mel Ferrer.

On screen and off, Audrey Hepburn has dressed at Givenchy since her movie Sabrina in 1954. "When I first went to Hubert," she explained later, "I was still in homemade dresses." A more simpatico meeting of two young talents would be hard to imagine—Givenchy the vanguard-man of contemporary chic; Hepburn the quintessence of never-before young elegance. On press day, though Givenchy himself was away, the staff received her not as a celebrity, but as an old friend of the house. She sat on the tiny sofa at the end of the big double salon which has, besides crystal chandeliers, some merciful little bright yellow fans high on the walls—a boon to the elbow-to-elbow audience.

The fashion news instantly began to flow: a series of linen dresses, some of them shaped, unbelted shirts; suits with deliciously contrasting rouleau belts, jackets shaped in front, loose at the back; perfect little seven-eighths and nine-tenths coats; a full range of oatmeal beige, and putty colours; impudent little black late-day dresses, high in front, low at the back with X-straps or drawstring décolletages. To Parisians china blue looked new; hem-bands on jackets, coats, dresses; curvy extended shoulders for set-in sleeves, and on sleeveless dresses. Miss Hepburn began to talk out her choices ("That little coat I'd like to have!" . . . "A lovely little dress. On Gloria Guinness it would be divine.") with comments from Mr. Ferrer, some sharp fashion, some pure-male-observer ("That's one idea for developing a non-existent bosom").

"I want to make some dream-choices for Vogue," declared Miss Hepburn sotto voce. "As if I were in a candy store." . . . The collection, a big one full of vivacity and excitement, swept on to the bride ("a gay one, a jazzy one"), and Vogue's crew with Miss Hepburn and Mr. Ferrer repaired to the top floor where Givenchy has his atelier. For two hours it was indeed a candy store as number after number was brought up for Miss Hepburn to look at, to try on, to consider. With professional deftness, she peeled in and out of perhaps fifty enchanting things, speeded from time to time by such Ferrer friendly persuasion as, "How about shucking into that white one." For Vogue she chose—because she has similar Givenchy clothes, would like to have them, or would like to wear them for a dream life without "the agony of suitcases"—ten looks photographed on pages 65 to 73, all with coiffures by Alexandre.

For herself she chose from this year's collection three things: two déshabillés and an evening dress. She also buys from Givenchy, as she needs them, enough suits to keep her working quota at two day suits—often beige or putty—plus one black one, coats picked to last for several seasons, late-day and evening dresses depending on the locale and timing of her movie plans.

When she's at home in Switzerland—a mountain top near Lucerne with a view of six lakes—she wears pants and sweaters. Pants and sweaters again when she's working every day, but a Givenchy déshabillé (perhaps shocking-raspberry linen) is "what I wear most in the evening when I'm working all day; it's a permissible dressing gown but elegant. I come home, have my bath, and put it on. Whether we have guests or not, I'm dressed."

Whether she is thinking for Hepburn-real or Hepburn-dream, it is vividly apparent that she chooses clothes with a sure eye for her proportion, an acute sense of fashion and a thorough understanding of herself within the Givenchy image. Her straight-from-the-heart summation: "I like him. I respect him. I admire him." ✳

---

OPPOSITE Audrey wearing a pink cloqué silk evening dress with her own shoes.

# { 10 }

# My Fair Lady Premiere

I n 1964, audiences everywhere were brimming with anticipation for the release of *My Fair Lady*, and Paris was no exception. The Broadway musical by Alan Lerner and Frederick Loewe had experienced a very profitable run in New York and on the West End in London but had never before graced the Paris stage. However, on one fateful winter's day, the French capital was finally granted the much-awaited opportunity to see George Cukor's Hollywood adaption of *My Fair Lady*. Audrey Hepburn and Rex Harrison arrived in Paris the week of Christmas for the premiere of their newest triumph.

After spending an arduous four and a half months filming at the Warner Brothers lot, Audrey and Rex graciously collected their laurels during their highly celebrated promotional tour. Before Paris, they attended the opening nights in New York, Chicago, San Francisco, and Los Angeles to warm applause. "I saw *My Fair Lady* ten times. That's rough," Audrey told reporter Mary Blume. "In New York, we thought we were pretty good, by Chicago we were crying in our beer."[116] Although the press tour began to wear on the talented actors, Audrey was counting down the days to the Paris premiere.

On December 19, 1964, Audrey and Rex attended a press conference in the lounge of the Hôtel Plaza Athénée located at 25 avenue Montaigne in the Eighth Arrondissement of Paris. Audrey wore a black sleeveless dress made of brocade silk from Givenchy's 1964 Winter collection. She neatly paired the cocktail dress with a set of Cartier diamond earrings (purchased in 1959) and elbow-length white gloves. The two costars made their way to the lounge, where they were greeted by a room packed with press. The room was elegantly constructed with wall-to-wall woodwork, an impressive marble fireplace, and tiered crystal chandeliers suspended from the ceiling. Audrey and Rex sat in large silk

OPPOSITE Audrey in her suite at the Ritz Paris getting ready for the *My Fair Lady* premiere. ABOVE Audrey and Rex Harrison in the lounge of the Hôtel Plaza Athénée.

chairs facing out toward a sea of French reporters who sat elbow to elbow. The journalists directed their questions at Audrey, who played the role of interpreter, translating Rex's answers from English to French. They asked her if she had taken singing lessons for the film, to which Audrey replied that she had taken a great many lessons. It was true; Audrey trained with singing coach Sue Seton, who helped her with her vocals for *My Fair Lady*. Together, Audrey and Sue spent hours on end, some days as many as eight hours, for five straight weeks preparing for the role of Eliza Doolittle. Despite their best efforts, the studio made the unfavorable decision to dub her vocals, opting to use professional-dubber-to-the-stars Marni Nixon.

ABOVE Roger Thiery styling Audrey's hair for the Paris premiere of *My Fair Lady*. OPPOSITE Audrey (wearing her sky blue Givenchy dress) and Mel dressing for the *My Fair Lady* premiere.

Two days later on December 21, Audrey visited Givenchy's atelier on 3 avenue George V for a dress fitting in which she tried on several different options including a long coat with a purple-and-pink floral motif (the same coat she had worn to the San Francisco premiere). The next day, on December 22, Audrey and Mel Ferrer were photographed in their suite at the Hôtel Ritz getting ready for the big premiere. Two photographers, Philippe Le Tellier from *Paris Match* magazine and Angela Williams, were hired to photograph the couple as they dressed in their evening attire. Also in the suite was Roger Thiery, Alexandre de Paris's assistant, who was styling Audrey's hair in one of his splendid upsweeps.

Audrey had been a longtime client of Alexandre de Paris since his original location at 11 rue du Faubourg Saint Honoré, which he shared with the well-known hairdressers the Carita sisters. Alexandre de Paris (birth name Louis Alexandre Raimon) was first introduced to Audrey in the spring

fashioning ornate hairstyles for their models to wear in fashion shows and photo shoots. In 1967, Audrey's longtime hairstylist at Alexandre's salon said, "In all my career, the greatest sensation I have had is Audrey Hepburn. On her one can see immediately the results of one's work."[117]

Audrey was a regular at his Paris salon and employed his talents whenever she needed her brunette locks styled for galas, premieres, movies, and numerous *Vogue* fashion shoots. Warner Brothers agreed to pay Alexandre and his team $2,000 to tend to Audrey's tresses for her *My Fair Lady* premieres. Audrey's statement hairdos were architectural and built high above her head. Her locks were gathered into oversized loops using a combination of Audrey's real hair and fake hairpieces that were layered and roped together, overpowering her small frame. The manicured coifs made quite the impression and were praised in newspapers and women's magazines. "Audrey's hair-do was the conversation piece of the evening,"[118] noted famed gossip columnist Hedda Hopper at the Hollywood screening of *My Fair Lady*. On the day of the Paris premiere, Roger fussed over the last touches of Audrey's elaborate updo before applying the final hairpin. With her hair and makeup in place, Audrey retired her silk robe for her arresting Givenchy gown.

Audrey's ensemble for the evening was a work of art by "The Gentleman Couturier," Monsieur de Givenchy. The sleeveless dress, from his 1964 Winter collection, was a beautiful shade of sky blue faconne brocade silk embroidered with crystals and delicate little fans sewn with metallic blue and silver silk threads. Worn over the floor-length gown was a matching capelet made of the same alluring motif. Giancarlo, a makeup artist from the Lancôme Beauty Institute in Paris, carefully applied Audrey's makeup for the occasion. Using only Lancôme products, he heavily lined her bottom and top lids with black liner and attached false lashes to create a dramatic eye framed by her signature full eyebrows. Audrey kept

of 1956 through their mutual friend, French fashion model Bettina Graziani. That summer, just before production began on *Love in the Afternoon*, Audrey would debut her new hairstyle, the *Paris Heart*. Although the hairstyle was originally created by American hairdresser Mr. Kenneth, Alexandre was hired to re-create her bob-length coiffure in Paris for publicity photos. Over the years, she continued to visit him at his new salon also located on rue du Faubourg Saint-Honoré, which he opened in 1957.

Alexandre de Paris was a French celebrity in his own right; he had a long list of international clients including the Duchess of Windsor, Begum Om Habibeh Aga Khan, Jackie Kennedy, Greta Garbo, Maria Callas, Lauren Bacall, and Elizabeth Taylor. He was the artist responsible for Liz's famous coiffure in the 1963 epic *Cleopatra*. He worked hand in hand with the top French haute couture designers,

ABOVE Audrey and Alexandre de Paris at Givenchy's Paris fashion show in March 1989. OPPOSITE Audrey and Hubert de Givenchy at Lasserre restaurant.

her accessories to a minimum; she chose her diamond Cartier earrings (the same ones she had worn two days earlier) and a pair of white Hermès opera gloves. She was a vision in blue.

On the evening of December 22, 1964, only three days before Christmas, 650 honored guests were invited to attend the Paris screening of *My Fair Lady*. The premiere was hosted at the Théâtre du Châtelet, an opera house located at Place du Châtelet in the First Arrondissement of Paris that had been designed by Gabriel Davioud and constructed between 1860 and 1862. The gala was given under the patronage of distinguished French magazines *Marie-Claire* and *Paris Match* and organized by publicity agent Georges Cravenne. All proceeds were given in benefit of Paris's most popular charity, Bal des Petits Lits Blancs, whose fete aboard the *France* cruise ship Audrey had attended only two years earlier.

Before the showing began, guests were treated to an elegant affair at five different three-star Paris restaurants: La Tour d'Argent, Lapérouse, Lasserre,

Le Grand Véfour, and Maxim's. Audrey and Mel made their way to Lasserre, located in the Champs-Elysées quarter in the Eighth Arrondissement. To accommodate the extensive guest list, each restaurant was delegated a host to preside over the evening's meal. At Lasserre, Audrey and Mel chaired separate tables while Rex Harrison feasted at La Tour d'Argent, located at 15 Quai de la Tournelle. On either side of Audrey sat her loyal friends Baron Guy de Rothschild and Hubert de Givenchy, both of whom looked handsome in their black tuxedos. Throughout the supper, as guests dined on fillets of sole and cockerels, friends and admirers made their way toward Audrey's table to toast her on her latest achievement. One offering her congratulations was Audrey's close confidante Countess Jacqueline de Ribes. Following dinner, Audrey and Mel were joined by couples on the dance floor. Once their courses were digested, Georges Cravenne organized a fleet of G7 taxis to transport the guests to the Théâtre du Châtelet.

Inside the packed theater, Rex Harrison and Mel Ferrer sat on either side of Audrey in their center seats in the orchestra section. Their chairs were garnished with feathers and flowers to set apart the esteemed costars from the rest of the room. Seated next to Rex was French businessman Jean Prouvost, owner of *Paris Match* magazine. The auditorium was overflowing with famous faces such as French actors Jean-Pierre Cassel and Françoise Dorléac and newlyweds German actress Elga Andersen and architect Christian Girard. Engaged in conversation were Italian actress Elsa Martinelli and Sophie Litvak, who was there with her husband, Anatole Litvak, Audrey's director from *Mayerling*. Also on the guest list was Audrey's *Love in the Afternoon* costar Maurice Chevalier and her dear friend Capucine, a French actress and former Givenchy model. Capucine's date for the evening was German playboy Gunter Sachs. It was said that Capucine had been in low spirits that day and debated whether to go to the premiere. Audrey rang her earlier in the afternoon to lend

some words of encouragement and later sent her chambermaid to Capucine's hotel with a large garment box from Maison Givenchy. Inside was a violet evening ensemble in brocade silk that Audrey had worn the previous season. Capucine arrived at the theater wearing the gown and matching coat and a pair of Bvlgari earrings also loaned from Audrey.

There was excitement in the air. The auditorium was buzzing with the sound of moviegoers mingling with their neighbors. Soon the lights dimmed and the audience fell silent. Audrey and Rex settled in to watch their movie for the umpteenth time. As the movie unfolded on-screen the audience expressed their enjoyment, cheering and applauding after each musical number. Once the final credits rolled on screen, Audrey and Rex were escorted to the proscenium; they fondly kissed each other on the cheek in front of a glowing crowd. It was another successful premiere for the real-life Eliza Doolittle and Henry Higgins.

Following the holidays, Audrey and Rex continued on their thriving *My Fair Lady* tour. Exactly one month later, on January 22, 1965, Audrey flew to London to attend the premiere at the Warner's Cinema in the West End. At the London premiere, Audrey was introduced to Princess Alexandra, the Honourable Lady Ogilvy, and her husband, Sir Angus Ogilvy. Other notable arrivals included Cecil Beaton, the costume designer of *My Fair Lady*; Jeremy Brett, the actor who played Freddy Eynsford-Hill; and actress Vivien Leigh. Once their publicity tour had concluded, Audrey returned to Paris in March to receive a new fashionable haircut at Alexandre de Paris's salon. She would show off her modern trim in her next film, *How to Steal a Million*, which would begin production that August in Paris. ✳

OPPOSITE TOP Audrey and Mel at the Théâtre du Châtelet. OPPOSITE BOTTOM Audrey and Mel arriving at the Théâtre du Châtelet for the premiere of *My Fair Lady*.

# { 17 }
# How to Steal a Million

It had been a year and a half since Audrey stepped foot on a movie set. The international press tour for *My Fair Lady* had kept her occupied and in dire need of a holiday. "I did a tour of the world practically for all the premieres of *My Fair Lady*," she griped to American gossip columnist Sheila Graham. "It was easier working in the picture than promoting it."[119] Audrey had worked incessantly since *Gigi*; she rarely took time for herself and was overtaxed from her constant work schedule. At thirty-six her priorities had changed. Sean was now five years old and starting school in Lausanne, Switzerland. Like his parents, he was already communicating in English, French, Italian, and Spanish. "Mel and I would like our son to have an international education. That way he'll learn to know all countries, and all peoples, and to grow up without prejudices,"[120] she told journalist Claude Berthod for *Cosmopolitan* magazine. To accommodate Sean's schooling, Audrey and Mel moved from their rental chalet in Bürgenstock and purchased a home in Tolochenaz, a quaint village near Lac Léman (a lake nestled between Lausanne and Geneva) in 1965. *La Paisible*, "The Peaceful," was a three-hundred-year-old Vaudois farmhouse built of pink-beige stone with a slated roof and blue shutters. La Paisible would quickly become Audrey's

sanctuary. Since she was a child she had aspired to own a home with a garden and ample space for her belongings: "I always dreamt of the day when I would have enough closets—big ones. Some people dream of having a big swimming pool—with me it's closets."[121] At La Paisible, she could have both.

La Paisible provided Audrey with the ordinary existence she had long desired. When asked to recount her day for *Cosmopolitan* magazine, Audrey described a day devoid of glamour: "I woke up at eight o'clock and went right to see Sean. I had coffee in bed. I got dressed. I read my mail. I worked a little around the house. I played with Sean and then we had lunch together. During his nap I made a few phone calls. Then the carpenter came to do some work and the bricklayer came to fix something in the courtyard. I took a long walk around the garden with the gardener and we discussed future plantings. When I got back I was cold, so I took a hot bath. I played with Sean and had dinner with him. I put him to bed. I called Mel, who is away for a few days. Then I went to bed myself and read a little before I went to sleep."[122] Although Audrey was enjoying the solitude of her new surroundings, she couldn't ignore that undeniable itch to act. After *My Fair Lady*, Audrey was all set for a comedy.

The movie was *How to Steal a Million Dollars and Live Happily Ever After*, more commonly known as *How to Steal a Million*. She would reunite with her *Roman Holiday* director, William Wyler, in Paris for a

---

OPPOSITE Audrey wearing her all-white three-piece suit with matching helmet hat and rounded sunglasses.

movie that could only be described as a fun fusion of romance, comedy, and a heist. *How to Steal a Million* was Hepburn and Wyler's third project together, after filming *Roman Holiday* in 1952 and working together on the 1961 black-and-white drama *The Children's Hour*. Audrey had a special affinity for Wyler. Like with Colette, she credited him for discovering her: "I think I was very lucky, because I was sort of Willy's baby," Audrey told the *Washington Post* in 1985. "He discovered me and nurtured me. He was very protective of me."[123] Wyler had become a paternal figure for Audrey, having watched her grow up on set: "I never saw her make a wrong move—professionally or personally. She's a real princess."[124]

After his last film, a psychological thriller called *The Collector*, Wyler was ready for a change in pace. *How to Steal a Million* told the story of a wealthy art collector, Charles Bonnet (Hugh Griffith), who paints and sells forgeries in the style of some of the world's best-known artists. Audrey plays Nicole

Bonnet, Griffith's conscientious daughter, who is less than enthused about her father's unfavorable profession. On the case is Simon Dermott (Peter O'Toole), the dashing art detective suspicious of Bonnet's illicit dealings. One night, Simon illegally enters the Bonnets' home with the intent to collect paint samples from Charles's forgeries when he is unexpectedly thwarted by an armed Nicole, dressed in a pink silk nightgown. Together Simon and Nicole devise a plan. Charles had recently loaned his fake Cellini *Venus* (insured for $1 million) to the Kléber-Lafayette Museum. Nicole, worried about her father's impending fate if the museum discovers the truth about his forgery, hires Simon to help her break into the museum and steal the statuette. The heist ensues and so does the on-screen chemistry between Audrey and Peter.

In the past, Audrey had been paired with leading men twice her age, but for the first time, she was coupled with a man three years her junior. Wyler

found the two to be effervescent together. Peter was charming, handsome, and a bit of a lush; but his on-set antics provided a sense of levity that Audrey soaked up. Peter had a mischievous sense of humor and loved a good teasing. On days when Audrey's energy started to slip, he would break out his imitations, causing her to "hold in my giggles until my stomach hurt."[125] "I thought [the] two would make an explosive team," Wyler professed, "but I never expected [them] to react to each other like laughing gas!"[126] There was an obvious ease between the two, which made for an enjoyable ride.

In March of 1965, before production began, Audrey made a quick stop at Alexandre de Paris's salon in Paris for a daring new trim. She had been growing out her hair since cutting it in 1958 for her movie *The Nun's Story*. (To illustrate her character's conversion into the sisterhood, Audrey [as Sister Luke] had bravely consented to having her hair cut on camera.) But after years of having long hair,

Audrey was in the mood for something more current, even a little radical. Any time Audrey altered her appearance, whether it was a fresh haircut, a change in makeup, or a new dress by Givenchy, it was written about in fashion magazines, and this time was no different. Her modern coif, the "Coupe Infante '66" (translated as "The Spanish Princess Haircut '66") made the pages of *Vogue*'s August 15, 1965, issue. The Coupe Infant '66 was a short cut worn straight just below the ears, with chunky sideburns, side-swept bangs, and a textured bouffant on top. William Klein photographed Audrey in a two-page spread debuting her new look and wearing the classic *traje corto* (a bullfighter's costume) she had worn at the *Feria de Abril*, a fair held each year in Seville, Spain. Alexandre had Audrey try on various

OPPOSITE Audrey and director William Wyler, photographed by Terry O'Neill. ABOVE Audrey and Peter O'Toole during the production of *How to Steal a Million*.

wigs before deciding on the cropped coiffure. *Vogue* described the process: "Alexandre then cut and set her hair four times before he arrived at the final enchantment he calls Coupe Infante '66 . . . Each strand is blunt-cut, then thinned diagonally with a razor from roots to ends, and finally polished with American scissors that cut on the bias—these are essential to the blending that gives this coif the look of a brisk little mane."[127] The results were *magnifique*!

The principal photography for *How to Steal a Million* commenced in July of 1965 in Paris at the Studios de Boulogne. Wyler employed the help of production designer Alexandre Trauner (who had

previously worked on *Love in the Afternoon*) to construct the fictional Kléber-Lafayette Museum, the Hôtel Ritz bar, and the interior of the Bonnet estate. Re-creating the Kléber-Lafayette Museum was an involved process. Trauner hired a young artist friend to paint reproductions of Monet, Rembrandt, Renoir, Van Gogh, Picasso, Miró, Delacroix, Degas, Gauguin, Goya, Matisse, Bonnard, and Staël to line the walls of the museum built entirely on a sound-stage. The young painter worked in a studio in the attics of the Boulogne reproducing sixty imitations for the film. Mr. Tamassi, another artist used by Trauner, sculpted the fake Cellini *Venus*, which O'Toole and Hepburn steal back with the help of a magnet and a boomerang.

The exterior of the Bonnets' mansion was located at 38 rue Parmentier in Neuilly-sur-Seine. The estate was the only private residence designed by French architect Charles Garnier, the architect

ABOVE Audrey on set of the Bonnets' mansion designed by production designer Alexandre Trauner. OPPOSITE TOP Peter and Audrey inspecting the artwork created by Trauner's artists. OPPOSITE BOTTOM Audrey outside the Bonnets' mansion in Neuilly-sur-Seine.

responsible for the Paris Opera House, and was later named for him, the Palais Garnier. The mansion was set for demolition, but after French officials saw the beautiful restoration paid for by Fox Studios there was an effort to save the property. The attempt was futile and the mansion was eventually torn down. Trauner also built a replica of NATO's military headquarters, where Audrey's character, Nicole, worked, only to have those scenes end up on the cutting room floor.

Hubert de Givenchy was put in charge of Audrey's wardrobe and given a generous budget of $30,000. Critics were speculating that Givenchy had fallen out of favor with the young public. The youthquake, a term coined in 1965 by *Vogue*'s editor in chief, Diana Vreeland, described the shift in pop culture pioneered by London's swinging generation. The movement had a major impact in fashion, seizing power from the French couture fashion houses that had reigned supreme. However, Audrey ignored the cynics. She and Hubert had worked successfully together for the past twelve years, developing a symbiotic relationship that carried off-screen. "We discovered each other," she said of her friendship with Givenchy. "There are few people that I love more. He is the single person I know with the greatest integrity."[128] When asked about his latest collection Audrey said, "I thought that it was sort of liquid and beautiful. In French, there is a word to describe it: 'Sobre.'"[129] In this instance, *sobre* meant "restrained."

Hubert designed twenty-four pieces for Nicole's Parisian wardrobe. His creations pulled influences from the happening *mod* (short for "modern") trend, exhibiting a playfulness and energy that audiences had not seen before. A report from the *Poconos Record* put it simply: "Givenchy's genius is at its unexcelled peak in the very fact that at no point does the costuming dominate the scene, impair the action or overpower either Miss Hepburn or the role she plays [ . . . ] The fashions

are keyed to accompany the unfolding of the story in the necessary but unobtrusive way a fine pianist accompanies a singer."[130]

In the opening scene of *How to Steal a Million*, Audrey is zipping along the Quai de l'Archevêché in a red Autobianchi Bianchina minicar wearing an all-white three-piece suit with matching futuristic helmet chapeau and white rounded Oliver Goldsmith sunglasses. The space-age style was all

he says, stunned. "You look, somehow, different." For this specific scene, Hubert designed a black Chantilly lace cocktail dress with matching jacket and lace stockings. The eye mask was a stroke of genius proposed by Audrey. This may have been one of the few times Audrey and Hubert disagreed on wardrobe. Hubert challenged the idea, arguing "I don't like face masks. Too carnival,"[131] but Audrey insisted. Nicole was dressed as *la femme fatale* and her veiled face achieved an air of mystery necessary for the scene. Audrey's stubbornness paid off; she looked ravishing and her lace ensemble soon became one of her most iconic looks. Of the twenty-four pieces commissioned for the film, Hubert created eye-catching outfits in mint green, hot pink, yellow, and navy, and a cream wool tunic coat with a blue-and-coral plaid print worn with a navy blue pillbox hat.

Audrey's transformation from 1950s ingénue to modern-day woman was incomplete without the help of her trusted makeup artist, Alberto de Rossi. At forty-nine, Alberto was considered the top makeup artist in Europe. He worked with some of Hollywood's most recognizable names, including Ava Gardner and Elizabeth Taylor. Little did Audrey know that when she first worked with Alberto on the set of *Roman Holiday*, she was gaining a lifelong friend. Alberto understood the facets of Audrey's face, and with his expert eye, he knew how to enhance her natural features: "Audrey's bones are photogenic. She has a very strong jawline. In a sense, I reversed her face by emphasizing her temples. Except for that, she has such beautiful bone structure that her features need very little shading."[132] Audrey was protective of her image and how she appeared in pictures and on film. For that reason, she was a loyal client, electing to work with the same photographers, cinematographers, and makeup artists time and again. Under Alberto's supervision, she felt safe; "I put myself entirely in the hands of my makeup man, Alberto de Rossi,

the rage with the haute couture designers, especially André Courrèges, Paco Rabanne, and Pierre Cardin, who in 1964 released his experimental "Cosmocorps" collection. Audrey looked seamless in her novel ensemble. Unlike some actresses who felt boxed in by fashion, Audrey was able to navigate the mainstream trends, adopting a style that was authentic to her.

In another scene filmed at the Hôtel Ritz (assembled by Trauner's team on a soundstage), Audrey wears her most seductive costume to date. She is beguiling in a head-to-toe lace ensemble with matching lace eye mask and lit cigarette. Simon does a double take when he sees Nicole waiting for him at the Ritz bar. "I didn't recognize you,"

ABOVE Audrey wearing her lace ensemble during the production of *How to Steal a Million*. OPPOSITE Audrey with her longtime makeup artist Alberto de Rossi.

whom I consider a real artist. I let him do what he likes and never look in a mirror all day."[133]

During the production of *How to Steal a Million*, Alberto's day began when Audrey arrived at her dressing room at 10:00 A.M. For an hour and a half, she would patiently sit while Alberto skillfully applied her makeup. Afterward, the two would leave for the studio together. While Audrey was busy acting, Alberto would wait in the wings, with his brushes in hand, ready to touch up the smallest of flaws. For her eyes, Audrey transitioned from her famed cat eye with a winged tip to a contemporary, outlandish look befitting of the progressive times. To create Audrey's heavy-lidded eye, Alberto would start by applying a pale shadow to both eyelids in an upward motion. Next, he would pencil delicately above the lid using a dark shade. With a small brush, Alberto would blend the lines until they became a transparent dark gray. He then applied a faint

layer of amethyst eye shadow. "Amethyst is subtle, like the shadow color of a vein," he explained. On Audrey's upper and lower lash lines, he heavily lined her eyes from the outer corner to the inner tear ducts. To complete the look, Audrey would coat her own eyelashes with mascara. Alberto would then add false eyelashes, "to add depth rather than length,"[134] and then apply one more layer of mascara. The result was dramatic and created the illusion that Audrey's eyes were twice as large and all the more expressive. For her lips he would use a natural or very light pink tint. Audrey's preferred shade was Silver Jonquil by Elizabeth Arden.

In the scene at the Ritz bar, Alberto used a silver pigmented shadow to create a metallic effect that shimmered in the light; the technique was used to draw attention to Audrey's eyes under her lace mask. "Those eyes of extravagant size behind a black tulle mask belong as much to Alberto de Rossi

as to Audrey Hepburn,"[135] wrote journalist Violette Leduc when she visited the set for *Vogue* magazine. The overall presentation played to Nicole's elusive demeanor. To add a finishing touch, Audrey wore oversize Cartier diamond earrings that glistened with the slightest tilt of her head. The stunning combination of Audrey's ultramodern haircut, Givenchy's modish wardrobe, and Alberto's artistry ushered Audrey into a new fashion era.

On hand to capture Audrey's metamorphosis was thirty-one-year-old Canadian photographer Douglas Kirkland. Kirkland had been hired by Twentieth Century Fox to shoot publicity stills for *How to Steal a Million*. He had first made a name for himself when he was assigned to

ABOVE AND OPPOSITE Audrey photographed by Kirkland in her Givenchy lace ensemble and metallic eye makeup.

photograph Marilyn Monroe for *Look* magazine in 1961. The images of Marilyn lying on a bed with nothing more than a white sheet between her and the camera became some of the most iconic photos of his career. In 1965, Kirkland was flown from America to Paris to shoot Audrey for the first time. Working with Audrey left an indelible impression on the photographer, as Kirkland would recall years later, "The atmosphere on a shoot was always very good with Audrey. She was professional and wanted to do what she could for the photographer. It meant that we were working very much in sync. She was always working for the camera. She knew what her best angles were, and when she came to our set for setup or stills, she was always prepared, ready, and on time with her wardrobe and hair done precisely. She was superb in every single way. Truthfully, I wish there were more Audrey Hepburns today."[136] During production, Kirkland snapped a series of photos of Audrey dressed in her Givenchy costumes posed in front of a solid backdrop at the Studios de Boulogne. The standout images of Audrey were vibrant close-ups highlighting the mastery of Alberto de Rossi's makeup and Alexandre de Paris's craftsmanship. Douglas's handiwork would become some of the most recognizable photos of Audrey's career.

Amid filming, Audrey still made time for her family and social events. On September 3, 1965, William Wyler, Audrey, Peter O'Toole, and Mel Ferrer arrived at the French premiere of Wyler's latest film, *The Collector* (*L'Obsédé* in French). *The Collector* received accolades in May when it opened at the Cannes film festival and took home the prizes for Best Actress (Samantha Eggar) and Best Actor (Terence Stamp). The screening was shown at Studio Publicis, a cinema located on avenue des Champs-Elysées. After the viewing, Audrey and Mel attended a private dinner honoring the movie's opening night.

On October 28, Audrey attended a ceremony for the 20th Nuit du Cinema at the Théâtre Marigny located at the crossing of Champs-Elysées and the avenue Marigny. Her date for the evening was her husband, Mel Ferrer, who had been preoccupied with work in Madrid and New York for his films *El Greco* and *Cabriola*. Audrey arrived in a pale blue shantung sleeveless gown by Givenchy with alternating panels embellished in a brocade detail. Over the dress, she wore a kimono-style evening coat in the same shade of blue. Dangling from her ears were a pair of diamond Cartier earrings that she had worn in a scene with Eli Wallach in *How to Steal a Million*. Audrey was awarded with the "Victoire" for Best Actress, a statuette equivalent to the American Oscar, for her performance in *My Fair Lady*. To present the award was actress Gina Lollobrigida, who acted as the evening's master of ceremony. Audrey received a standing ovation when she accepted her statuette onstage. Seated in the balcony section next to the Ferrers were their dear friends and the function's chairs, Prince Rainier III and his wife, the Princess of Monaco (formerly known as the actress Grace Kelly). Guests included Jean Marais, Peter O'Toole, Claude Dauphin, Louis de Funès, Marie-José Nat, Françoise Sagan, and her ex-husband, Bob Westhoff.

On her weekends off, Audrey would take a forty-five-minute flight to Switzerland to visit Sean, who was staying at home with his nanny in Tolochenaz. On one special afternoon, she brought Sean to Paris to enjoy a day at the Cirque d'Hiver. Sean marveled at the animated acrobats and clowns. After the show Sean was interviewed by a reporter. He affirmed that although his mother had been frightened when a tiger jumped on an elephant, he remained unafraid.

Before production wrapped on *How to Steal a Million*, a cocktail party was given at the Studios de Boulogne to exhibit the impressive collection of forged paintings created by Trauner's team of artists. Audrey arrived late to the party and was greeted with a friendly kiss by O'Toole. She had traded in her plain blue smock (from a scene she had filmed earlier that day) for her black lace Givenchy dress sans mask. The party had been organized by Twentieth Century Fox to celebrate the end of filming—despite the fact that the film was a week behind schedule. Many members of Parisian society and the film industry were invited, including Monsieur Coutela, a security guard hired by Cartier to protect a $300,000 engagement ring loaned from the renowned jewelers for the movie. Coutela happily sat in a corner enjoying a glass of champagne and his snacks. Seen inspecting the paintings was the president of Fox, Darryl Zanuck, who was photographed with a large cigar in one hand and a mysterious blonde in the other. When a reporter stopped Peter O'Toole to ask why he was skulking about the room, he cryptically replied that he was avoiding everyone.

Filming concluded in early December. Audrey was already signed on to her next film, *Two for the Road*, a romantic comedy/drama directed by her *Funny Face* and *Charade* director, Stanley Donen. The film would bring her back to the French capital in May, but until then Audrey would return home to La Paisible to spend quality time with her family. During their free days, Audrey and Mel frequented Spain, where they were building a house in Marbella near their good friend, actress Deborah Kerr, who had also purchased a property close by. *How to Steal a Million* wasn't a commercial success, but it charmed audiences. As Marjory Adams noted in her review for the *Boston Globe*, "It is probably Audrey Hepburn's most amusing and satisfying comedy since she made *Roman Holiday* in 1953 for the same Mr. Wyler."[137] ✳

# Two for the Road

Nineteen sixty-six started off as a somber year for the thirty-seven-year-old actress. In 1965, while filming *How to Steal a Million*, Audrey discovered that she was pregnant and due in June the following year. The happy mother-to-be was overjoyed by the unexpected news; she had prayed for a second child since Sean's arrival in 1960, but her dreams were quickly dashed. In January of 1966, Audrey suffered another miscarriage and the heartbreak was more than she could bear. Her name was already attached to Stanley Donen's newest project, *Two for the Road*, but after learning she was pregnant, she had every intention of declining. The script was a drastic detour from her past performances; the subject matter was mature and delved into the dissection of a marriage. Audrey, still recovering from her loss, deferred to Mel for his opinion. In the past, Mel had remedied Audrey's bouts of depression by distracting her with work, and this time was no different. He could see how the film industry was evolving and sensed that *Two for the Road* would be an excellent vehicle for Audrey's updated image. At Mel's encouragement, Audrey agreed to keep the role. The movie was set to film that spring in May in the South of France and Paris. Time away in the sun might be exactly what the doctor ordered.

OPPOSITE Audrey on the set of *Two for the Road*.

*Two for the Road* was written by Academy Award–winning screenwriter Frederic Raphael. After watching *Nothing But the Best*, Donen reached out to Raphael in hopes of collaborating on Donen's next picture. Raphael pitched an idea he had been mulling over, inspired by the road trips he and his wife would take in the South of France. *Two for the Road* is an examination of a modern marriage, spanning over twelve years. "[The movie] starts in 1966, jumps back to 1954, cuts ahead to 1958, back to 1956, forward to 1963, and so on,"[138] Donen explains. The story follows the lives of architect Mark Wallace and his wife, Joanna, as they drive through the South of France in five different time periods. The plot moves back and forth, starting from when they first meet as unattached twentysomethings, skipping ahead to present day, then showing a married couple on the verge of divorce. "You haven't been happy since the day we met, have you?" Joanna laments to Mark. Donen shrewdly uses different models of cars to guide the audience throughout the nonlinear timeline, beginning with a Volkswagen Minibus in 1954, followed by a Ford Country Squire for 1956, a green MG TD for 1958, a red Triumph Herald for 1963, and a white Mercedes-Benz 230SL for the year 1966. The alternating jumps through time reveal the deterioration of their marriage through humor, bitter squabbles, extramarital affairs, and what were once considered happier times.

"It is inconceivable that it could have been submitted to me ten years ago, even five," Audrey rationalized.[139] Before this film, audiences weren't ready to watch the unblemished star portray a character that uses profanity, commits adultery, and partakes in her first on-screen love scene. "It treats adultery frankly and that in itself is a refreshing change because nobody is dreadfully punished in the last reel. Because there is no awful penance extracted from anyone at the end of the picture it doesn't make the adultery any less tragic. Adultery is always tragic. And that is just the way it is in this story. But there is much that is funny, tender and rather wonderful about marriage and these ingredients are all there too."[140] The nuanced material allowed Audrey to exhibit her refined acting chops as a wife trapped in a broken marriage. In Joanna's skin, she was able to shed her image as the perennial ingenue.

Thirty-year-old English actor Albert Finney played Audrey's on-screen husband. Albert Finney had made a name for himself in the 1964 movie *Tom Jones*. Following his success on the big screen, he had taken a fifteen-month hiatus to perform onstage in England's National Theater. It wasn't until he read the script for *Two for the Road* that Finney contemplated a return to films, and a large part of that was due to his costar. Finney professed that he had always wanted to work with Audrey and, frankly, who could blame him? Audrey and Albie, as his friends called him, had an undeniable connection. With Albie, she let down her defenses. She was silly, lighthearted, and even flirtatious. According to Donen, the chemistry between Audrey and Albie was palpable: "The Audrey of the last few weeks on this film I didn't even know. She overwhelmed me. She was so free, so happy. I never saw her like that. So young! I don't think I was responsible, flattering as that thought would be. I guess it was Albie."[141]

Novelist Irwin Shaw, who was visiting the set, also observed the magnetism between the two

ABOVE Audrey and Albert Finney as their characters Joanna and Mark. OPPOSITE Audrey with the *Two for the Road* film crew at a beach in St. Tropez.

actors. "She and Albie have this wonderful thing together, like a pair of kids with a perfect understanding and a shorthand of jokes and references that close out everybody else," he told *Ladies Home Journal*. "When Mel was there it was funny. Audrey and Albie got rather formal and a little awkward, as if now they had to behave like grown-ups."[142] Similar to their characters in *Two for the Road*, Audrey and Albie began an on-set affair. Tensions had been growing for some time between Audrey and Mel. Outwardly, they projected a happy marriage but behind closed doors there was discord at home. The public had been speculating about their marriage since their wedding in 1954, claiming that Mel was overbearing and too protective of his wife.

The press often compared their dynamic to the fictional characters Svengali and Trilby, accusing Mel of exercising too much control over Audrey's life and career. Friends and family never warmed to Mel, including Audrey's mother, the baroness, who firmly opposed their wedding from the start. And whether or not it was intentional, Audrey would sometimes hint at Mel's temper. "He can be very angry at times, and that may be a fault. But he can contain himself,"[143] she revealed to journalist David Stone in 1956. However, Audrey valued her privacy and fervidly denied the media's claims. Having never recovered from the wounds of her parents' divorce and her father's absence, Audrey admittedly held on to the marriage for the sake of

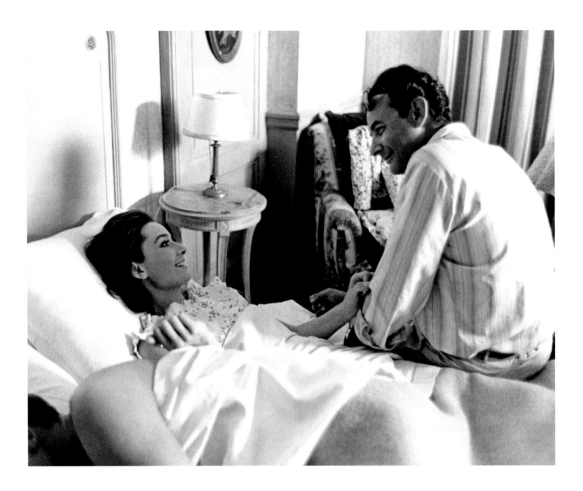

Sean. But over time the Ferrers' relationship began to unravel and both were accused of infidelity. The truth of the matter was, Audrey and Mel were headed toward divorce.

But for four blissful months, traveling around France, Audrey was able to detach from her current reality and seek warmth in the arms of her handsome new friend. "I love Albie," she gushed. "Oh, I really do. He's so terribly, terribly funny. He makes me laugh like no one else can. And you can talk to him. Really talk. He's serious, too, completely so about acting. And that's wonderful. Albie's just

ABOVE Audrey discussing a scene with director Stanley Donen.

plain wonderful, that's all there is to it."[144] The attraction between the two was more than casual, as Albert Finney would later describe: "Audrey and I met in a seductive ambience [in] a very sensual time in the Mediterranean. We got on immediately. After the first day's rehearsals, I could tell that the relationship would work out wonderfully. [ . . . ] During a scene with her, my mind knew I was acting but my heart didn't, and my body certainly didn't! Performing with Audrey was quite disturbing, actually . . . With a woman as sexy as Audrey, you sometimes get to the edge where make-believe and reality are blurred. [ . . . ] The time spent with Audrey is one of the closest I've ever had."[145] They were like two teenagers in love. Audrey's shift in attitude manifested on film, her smile was twice as bright and her laughter filled the screen. Albie was her antidote.

A caravan of trucks, buses, and trailers (many of which were carrying Audrey's sizable wardrobe) moved throughout France, settling in Saint-Tropez, the French Riviera, Côte d'Azur, Nice, Cap Valéry, and Paris. Donen and his hundred-member production team turned a three-thousand-ton ferryboat, the *Cyrnon*, stationed at Port de Nice, into a temporary floating studio. In the film, Joanna and Mark meet for the first time as young travelers aboard the ferry. Mark has misplaced his passport and Joanna finds it tucked in his luggage, a running gag that continues throughout the movie. On board the *Cyrnon*, the cast and crew hosted a belated birthday celebration for Audrey. They sang "Happy Birthday" and presented her with a forty-pound four-tiered chocolate layer cake. The cake was lined with little flowers made of frosting and decorated with the titles from Audrey and Stanley's movies: *Funny Face*, *Charade*, and *Two for the Road*.

Donen went to great lengths to get his shots. To avoid disturbing the natural rhythm of his actors, he had three cameras rolling at all times. He carefully hid cameras in the sand, under rocks, and dangling from trees. He and his crew would be waist-high in the ocean with a large standing camera attached to a floating platform specially designed for the job. Donen created a relaxed environment on set. At 8:00 A.M. the crew (made up of electricians, a script supervisor, assistants, and prop men) would slowly roll in before the lead actors arrived. Audrey kept to a strict schedule: in bed by 9:00 P.M., up at 7:00 A.M., pickup at 9:15, followed by hair and makeup at 9:30 and a call time around noon. When the cast and crew weren't on the secluded beaches of Saint-Tropez or poolside at a private home in Var, France, they were in Paris filming the interior shots at Franstudio in Joinville and Billancourt Studios in Boulogne-Billancourt.

During *Two for the Road*, Audrey partook in her first on-screen love scene. Keeping with the times, the scenes themselves were modest, exposing very little. The script called for two separate shots. The first scene depicts Joanna and Mark intimate for the first time after hitchhiking around France. Covered by a bedsheet, all that is shown are Audrey's bare arms and upper back. "This is definitely against my principles," Mark declares. "Good," Joanna whispers. "I wouldn't like to think it happened all the time." The second occurred during the 1963 timeline and was filmed at Le Golf Hotel (now Le Beauvallon) in Saint-Tropez. Imaginably, Audrey was anxious. To alleviate her nerves, Twentieth Century Fox rented out the entire hotel and closed off the building to all members but the lighting crew, cameramen, Stanley Donen, and his production assistant.

A key component to the storytelling of *Two for the Road* and "The beginning of the new-look Hepburn,"[146] as Audrey put it, was Joanna's wardrobe. The switch in Audrey's wigs and clothes were integral to the time jumps, helping to guide the audience over the twelve-year time span. From the start, Donen informed Audrey that he didn't want Givenchy for costumes. He was adamant that Givenchy's clothes were too chic for an architect's wife. It was essential to Donen to preserve a sense of realism among his characters. Audrey was undoubtedly disappointed. In an attempt to change his mind, she invited Donen to Givenchy's Paris showroom to view his latest collection. Donen's response was "Smashing but wrong. We will find your wardrobe in boutiques."[147] And that's exactly what they did.

Previously, all of Audrey's costumes had been custom-made either by Givenchy or the studio's wardrobe department; just the thought of shopping in boutiques overwhelmed her. For the last thirteen years, Audrey had depended on Givenchy's polished designs for her more glamorous roles. With

Hubert in charge of wardrobe, Audrey could gladly avoid the long hours spent standing for multiple fittings and trying on clothes in cramped fitting rooms. Throughout the course of their relationship, Hubert used only one clothes mannequin for Audrey. The mannequin, which was stored in his workroom, was fit to her specific measurements and never budged an inch. From 1953 until her death in 1993, Audrey maintained the same svelte physique. But to keep up with the changing times, Audrey had to make some sacrifices.

Her tour of prêt-à-porter shops began in Paris. Mel Ferrer and Stanley Donen escorted Audrey to different boutiques with the newest ready-to-wear fashions, but the outing didn't last long. Audrey became more discouraged with each shop they entered. She quickly grew tired and returned to her hotel room, leaving the two men in charge. "You two know what's right for me," she said to Donen and her husband. "You do the shopping. I'll try on whatever you bring me. But in a nice, comfortable hotel suite."[148] Mel and Stanley knew that persuading Audrey was a fruitless endeavor, so they continued on without her. "We raced through about twelve boutiques like madmen. Heaven knows what the salesgirls thought,"[149] Mel proclaimed. The early birds arrived before the shops opened and pulled pieces from practically every clothing rack, yelling to each other across the store. By noon, they were exhausted. They had purchased a total of ninety different articles of clothing and took them back for Audrey to inspect. From the ninety items, Audrey chose a selection of twenty-nine pieces. The two men considered it a victory.

However, the search for Audrey's wardrobe wasn't complete. Stanley passed the baton to his wife, Adele Donen, a stylish American who was well known in high society. Adele had recently *gone*

OPPOSITE Audrey in her "ready-to-wear" fashions from *Two for the Road.*

*boutique* herself. The transition to boutique dressing was all the rage in fashion and a major adjustment for women who were staunch haute couture customers. Even famous French designers like Yves Saint Laurent, a favorite of Mrs. Donen, were creating ready-to-wear lines. Saint Laurent was one of the first couturiers to open his own ready-to-wear boutique under the name Saint Laurent Rive Gauche in September of 1966. Givenchy followed suit and in 1968 launched his own ready-to-wear line, Givenchy Nouvelle Boutique. Marc Bohan, Saint Laurent's successor after he left Dior in 1960, launched Miss Dior in 1967. The industry was advancing and fast. At only sixteen years old, a young English fashion model by the name of Twiggy was declared "the Face of '66." A slip of a girl with cropped blond hair and mammoth eyes had taken the modeling industry by storm. The lengths of hemlines had been hiked up from mid-calf to well above the knee, and radical colors and prints were popping up in every collection. Mod fashion was everywhere. Having originated out of London, the modern styles were creeping up all over Europe and the United States.

Joining Audrey's team as a fashion consultant was Lady Clare Rendlesham, the former editor of London's *Queen* magazine, who recalled, "I gathered together, from London and Paris, some 70 outfits and brought them to Stanley at his hotel. Audrey flew into Paris from Switzerland, tried on clothes all day, and took the last plane of the day out of Paris back home to Switzerland. I've never seen anything like her professionalism. She's not all that easy to dress, either. The lines have to be just so. She likes all the sweaters and blouses taken in almost like skin. It was very new for her, wearing an outfit that came straight off the peg for only seventeen guineas."[150] Similar to the manic shopping spree Stanley and Mel had undertaken, Mrs. Donen and Lady Clare Rendlesham swept through everything the French and English markets had to offer.

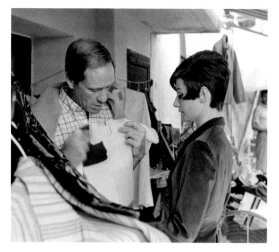

midwesterner originally from Fort Wayne, Indiana. After graduating from Parsons School of Design in Manhattan he left for Paris to make a living as a painter before opening a textile factory called Falconetto in Milan. He gradually began creating dresses with his own fabrics and selling them to the Italian ready-to-wear market. His loose-fitting dresses were made of brightly colored prints in cotton, chiffon, or silk jersey with long flowing trumpet sleeves. Barbra Streisand was captured by Richard Avedon wearing one of Scott's designs on the cover of *Vogue*'s March 15, 1966, issue. Later that year, in October of 1966, Scott would open his first boutique in Paris at 4 rue de la Paix.

Audrey spent two days with Scott at his Milan showroom. "From the outset Audrey had very firm, not to say rigid, ideas about how she should be dressed," Scott explained. "No bright colors. Above all, no prints. She said they would take away from her face. Can you imagine—Audrey Hepburn, with her head, worried about a dress upstaging her? She was fine about the swimsuits, though. Audrey is, well, a very slim girl indeed, and she agreed right away when I suggested a small amount of padding."[151] He submitted twenty-eight designs, of which Audrey chose twelve. He also designed custom-made shirts in solid colors and stripes, colorful plastic dangling earrings, and three one-piece bathing suits in red, black, and a colorful psychedelic pattern. In a scene from *Two for the Road*, Mark and Joanna are pulling up in front of the fictional Hotel Domaine Saint-Just in their white Mercedes-Benz 230. Joanna is changing out of her orange Cacherel shirt and white Courréges cotton skirt into Ken Scott's tent-shaped dress in a multicolor pastel print with bell-shaped sleeves and a hemline way above the knee. This popular silhouette was Scott's signature style. "As soon as his dresses come in, they walk right out of the store,"[152] said Third Avenue boutique owner Jerry Goldfarb to the *New York Times*.

Yet their assignment had only just begun. Audrey made an impressive 150 wardrobe changes in *Two for the Road*, and still they were in need of more options. It was at Adele Donen's suggestion that Audrey met with forty-seven-year-old American fashion designer Ken Scott. He was making waves in Milan with his colorful printed dresses that were drawing comparisons to Pucci, a successful Italian fashion brand. Scott was a

ABOVE Audrey and Mel clothes shopping in the French Riviera.

Adele Donen arranged for Audrey to meet with another up-and-coming designer, Paco Rabanne. Rabanne (birth name Francisco Rabaneda Cuervo) was a thirty-two-year-old Spanish-born designer based out of Paris. He studied architecture at l'École Nationale des Beaux-Arts, eventually finding success as a leading fashion designer in the "space age" phenomenon. Prior to venturing out on his own, he began his career as a jewelry designer creating pieces for the haute couture houses including Givenchy, Balenciaga, and Dior. In 1964, Rabanne caused a stir when he presented his first collection, "Twelve Experimental Dresses." He followed the success of his experimental collection by launching his own couture house in 1966. His debut couture collection was fittingly called "Twelve Unwearable Dresses." Rabanne was fascinated by unconventional materials. His micromini dresses were made of aluminum, metal, and plastic discs. They were strung together, not with a needle and thread, but with eight different pliers, liquid glue, and metallic rings. Rabanne's cutting-edge designs were the talk of Paris and his name was splashed across the pages of *Vogue*.

Audrey traveled to Rabanne's rooftop workrooms at 29 rue du Caire in Paris to try on one of his "unwearable dresses." (She confessed the dress was uncomfortable to sit in.) Of his creations, Audrey chose a thigh-length sheath dress made of silver spangled plastic discs worn over a nude body stocking. The snazzy futuristic dress was perfect for a scene featuring a 1966 cocktail party set in Saint-Tropez. The scene was filmed on a soundstage at Franstudio in Joinville, on the outskirts of Paris. The sardonic couple arrives at Mark's newly constructed home belonging to one of his clients. The architecturally modern house, complete with sunken living room, adds to the fabulously chic ambience of the soiree. Guests are sipping champagne and grooving along to the jazzy tunes of Henry Mancini breezily playing in the background. Audrey shimmies around in her metallic armored sheath with matching shoulder-length earrings. The dress moves with ease as the light reflects off the individual celluloid discs, perfect for the dress that Rabanne describes as not for sitting but for dancing.

Audrey also relied on the talents of Michèle Rosier, the designer for the French ready-to-wear house V de V (short for *Vêtements de Vacance*). Rosier was nicknamed the "Vinyl Girl" for her use of plastics and was recognized as the premier designer who introduced vinyl to Paris. In a scene shot at Le Golf Hotel's beach clubhouse, Audrey wears a yellow vinyl jacket with clear vinyl cutouts and matching yellow shorts. Sheltering her face from the sun is a pair of white wraparound Yuhu sunglasses by Oliver Goldsmith. Audrey also selected a lubricious black vinyl pantsuit over a pink, black, and white silk button-down shirt by Cacharel, a French prét-à-porter brand founded in 1962 by Jean Bousquet. Audrey was so pleased with Cacharel's shirts that she kept the five worn in the film and bought additional shirts for her personal wardrobe.

Adele Donen also insisted that Audrey wear the clothes of London-based designer Mary Quant. Mary Quant was a crucial figure in the inception of the mod fashion movement. Audrey chose two shirt dresses by "The Mother of Mod," a long-sleeved red-and-yellow-striped jersey shift and a green jersey minidress with a white zip-up collar. In the final scene of the film, Joanna and Mark are driving through French customs on their way to Italy. Keeping with the ongoing theme, Mark once again misplaces his passport. Joanna coolly attaches it to the steering wheel of their white Mercedes. Mark smiles and affectionately says, "bitch" to which Audrey lovingly responds, "bastard." Wearing her Mary Quant green-and-white dress, Audrey abandons her good girl image with that one simple word.

Patricia Thomas, a London hairdresser, flew to Paris to help with Audrey's wigs and swinging new hairstyles. "It's always a little tricky doing any new customer's hair for the first time, you know. And

with someone like Audrey Hepburn who has such a clearly defined image, it was perhaps even more difficult. Audrey was very concerned about keeping a small, neat head. She's right, of course. It suits her perfectly,"[153] Patricia explained. They selected four styles and sent them to an Italian wigmaker to create customized versions for the film. Grazia de Rossi tended to Audrey's hair on set and her husband, Alberto de Rossi, the man responsible for Audrey's iconic eyes, was hired to do her makeup. "I modified her eyebrows for this film. Of course, you don't notice. Very, very subtle. They're twice as thin now as when she made her first film. Then they were immense—but you never noticed how I brought them down, film by film. I've given her completely new eyes for this film. Very, very subtle."[154] In the long run, the extensive hours of clothes shopping, wig fittings, and multiple trips to Paris proved worthwhile. The result: Audrey's ultimate on-screen metamorphosis.

*Two for the Road* wrapped in September 1966. Audrey and Albie parted ways after filming, leaving behind tender memories from their time on set. The Ferrers flew to the United States to begin production on Audrey's next film, *Wait Until Dark*. Audrey played a blind woman tormented by a brutish Alan Arkin in her New York apartment. Mel signed on as a producer—this would be their last time working together, as in 1967, after completing *Wait Until Dark*, Audrey and Mel announced their separation. "In 13 years of living together, some dissension is inevitable. But I will not destroy what was between us with bitter words or memories,"[155] Audrey told the press before returning home to Switzerland to be with her son. Then on November 20, 1968, after fourteen years of marriage, Audrey filed for divorce in Morges, Switzerland. By this point, Audrey's tune had significantly changed: "I have spent two years in hell, surely the worst of my life."[156] In the divorce,

finalized in December, Audrey received custody of Sean; the two continued to live at Audrey's Swiss home, La Paisible. In the years after their marriage, Audrey and Mel spoke only a handful of times when it related to their son, Sean.

However, the solitude of the Swiss mountains quickly began to feel isolating for the new divorcée. Audrey escaped to Paris to spend time with friends as she recovered from this difficult period. She took comfort in the company of Hubert de Givenchy and actress Deborah Kerr. On March 4, 1968, while separated from Mel, she had attended the opening of Givenchy's new ready-to-wear boutique at 66 avenue Victor Hugo in Paris. The following week Audrey was photographed by Eve Arnold for a special UNICEF (United Nations Children's Fund) assignment. She interviewed a Jewish refugee who tearfully recounted his journey from Morocco to Paris in his pursuit to flee anti-Semitism, a reality Audrey knew all too well from her time in the Netherlands during World War II.

It would be nearly a decade before Audrey made another film. Her life was in transition; she was a single mother who was ready to leave acting, a profession that had dominated the last sixteen years of her life. During the summer of 1968, while cruising with friends around the Greek islands, Audrey met a young Italian psychiatrist nine years her junior. On January 18, 1969, only six weeks after her divorce was finalized, Audrey and Andrea Dotti tied the knot during a small ceremony at the town hall in Morges, Switzerland. Audrey was closing a significant chapter in her life and embarking on a new adventure. Together with Sean, Audrey and Andrea settled in Rome to begin their lives as newlyweds. ✳

OPPOSITE Audrey wearing her "unwearable" silver disc Paco Rabanne dress.

# { 19 }
# Soirees at the Rothschilds

I t had been four years since the premieres of *Two for the Road* and *Wait Until Dark* in 1967. In that time, Audrey had successfully avoided the burning spotlight cast from the hills of Hollywood and found happiness in the Italian capital of Rome. In 1971, at the age of forty-two, Audrey had gracefully shifted from international movie star to Signora Dotti, wife of Dr. Andrea Dotti, and full-time stay-at-home mother to her two sons. Her title as *Mum* was her most rewarding role yet. Sean was now ten and living in Rome with Audrey, Andrea, and their newborn son—on February 8, 1970, a year after her wedding, Audrey had given birth to her second son, Luca Dotti. For years, Audrey had struggled to have another child. Despite having spent the duration of her pregnancy on bed rest at the advice of her doctor, Audrey couldn't have been happier to finally fulfill her dream of giving Sean a sibling.

Fatigued from the hustle and bustle of Hollywood, Audrey was content spending her days catering to her family. Her mornings were devoted to her sons and the evenings were dedicated to her husband, who split his time between working at his private practice and the hospital Policlinico Umberto I. "When he's on night duty, I go down there sometimes and take him a meal and sit with him a bit,"[157] she shared with her friend of twenty years, journalist Henry Gris. At the hospital she wasn't "Audrey Hepburn"; she was simply known as Dr. Dotti's wife. "My life is filled with affection," she happily expressed to Gris. "Andrea is a terribly sweet-tempered, kind man. Full of fun. Very bright. And my children are my joy, of course. Sean is a big, healthy, sweet boy who is enormously tall. He is just 10 and looks 14. And I've made this other one and he is so very alert and very sweet and a beautiful baby. He looks very much like Andrea."[158]

One would think that after years of traveling abroad, shooting pictures in Paris, New York, Los Angeles, and even the Belgian Congo, Audrey would grow tired of her slower-paced existence, but quite the opposite was true. She had fully assimilated into her life of leisure. She was now your everyday Roman woman. She did her own grocery shopping, socialized with her group of Italian friends, entertained her husband and his associates, and, now and again, dipped her toe in the local nightlife. She also fully embraced the Italian fashion scene: "I hear [Givenchy] has a beautiful collection this year. Not that I'll see it. I now shop mostly in Rome, in our boutiques, and they're quite beautiful."[159] The couturier and his muse were still very much attached at the hip, but Audrey's commitment to becoming a full-time Roman meant that certain aspects of her life were bound to change. She traded in her Parisian haute

---

OPPOSITE Audrey, wearing her Valentino gown, photographed by Cecil Beaton for a *Vogue* feature titled "Remembrance of Things Proust."

couture gowns for the designs of a young Italian couturier, Valentino Garavani. Although her life on the outside looked considerably different from the woman the world once knew, Audrey had not abandoned her former self. She continued to move in the same social circles and book her seasonal sojourns to Paris. In December of 1971, Audrey and Andrea flew to Paris to attend the annual ball of the season thrown by her close friends Baron Guy and Marie-Hélène de Rothschild.

The Rothschild family was an integral part of European aristocracy. Their prestigious rise had begun in the eighteenth century, when Mayer Amschel Rothschild established the family banking business in Germany. After his death, he left his enterprise to his five sons, who established branches in Frankfurt, Vienna, London, Naples, and Paris, ensuring the family's financial status as titans of banking. The Rothschilds moved in influential circles and consorted with European

nobility, including Napoleon III. Mayer's son, James Mayer de Rothschild (who moved to Paris in 1812 and opened the French branch, De Rothschild Frères, in 1817), would host shooting parties for Napoleon III on his French estate, Château de Ferrières. Ferrières, located thirty miles east of Paris, was constructed between 1855 and 1859 and was built by the famous English architect Joseph Paxton, the man responsible for designing the Crystal Palace in London. Set on a thousand acres, the château was seized by Germans during the occupation of France and left abandoned—until 1959 when Baron Guy de Rothschild and his new bride, Baroness Marie-Hélène de Rothschild, restored the estate for their personal use. Château de Ferrières would become the site for some of Paris's most ostentatious societal balls, including the Bal Proust in 1971.

Audrey was first introduced to Guy and Marie-Hélène in the 1950s and she was often seen with the Rothschilds at society events around Paris. They had accompanied Audrey and her then-husband Mel Ferrer to *The Longest Day* premiere at the Palais de Chaillot and the Paris premiere of

ABOVE LEFT Audrey and her husband, Andrea Dotti, at their home in Rome, 1969. ABOVE RIGHT Audrey with her son, Luca Dotti, at La Paisible in Switzerland, 1971.

*My Fair Lady*. In their stylish designer threads, Guy, Marie-Hélène, and Audrey would gather to watch the horse races at the Hippodrome de Longchamp, a popular racecourse located at route des Tribunes at the Bois de Boulogne in Paris. The trio of friends would remain close throughout the years, and after the Ferrers divorced, the baron and baroness would continue to invite Audrey to Château de Ferrières with her new husband.

On December 2, 1971, an international guest list consisting of 350 influential people arrived at a dimly lit facade illuminated only by the ornate eight-branched crystal chandeliers glowing from the windows of the three-floor estate. Baron and Baroness Guy de Rothschild were hosting their annual ball for their exclusive group of friends. Among the crowd were renowned artists, royalty, members of nobility, celebrities, and the affluent members of European society. Every year the Rothschilds chose a theme for their elaborate party and this year's was "A Remembrance of Things Past," in honor of the famous novel by Marcel Proust, *À la recherche du temps perdu*. It was the centennial of Proust's birth in 1871, and attendees were informed that they should dress in accordance with the ball's theme.

Chauffeured limousines drove up the long driveway leading to the main entrance of Château de Ferrières. Women wearing their finest silks, furs, and diamonds were accompanied by men in black tuxedos and white ties and greeted by footmen dressed in red Louis XV livery and powdered wigs. Entering the foyer, the guests were shown to a large table displaying 350 place cards assigning each person a table number and name. The men and women, dressed in costumes faithful to the time period, were led by footmen carrying candelabras up the L'escalier d'Honneur, the main double staircase. On the steps were eighteen violinists scoring the evening's soiree. Three main salons were opened to the esteemed guests.

Standing in the Salon des Tapisseries was Baron Guy de Rothschild, dressed in tails and a fake white mustache, and his wife, Marie-Hélène, who looked lovely in an Yves Saint Laurent pearl white satin gown detailed with black satin bows on each sleeve. Her curled blond locks were flowered with satin roses and black velvet bows.

Upon their arrival, actress Elizabeth Taylor and her husband, actor Richard Burton, were escorted by Baron Alexis de Redé, a longtime friend of the Rothschilds. Elizabeth, dripping in diamonds and emeralds worth $3 million, wore an extravagant one-thousand-gem headdress designed by the prominent Paris jewelers Van Cleef & Arpels. Her coiffure was created by none other than Alexandre de Paris, the hairdresser of the night. The headdress was set with twenty-five pear-cut diamonds and gently draped over the actress's forehead. Her hair was woven with black roses and green velvet leaves, and erupting from the top was a 20-carat emerald set in black aigrette feathers. Her Valentino dress was of black taffeta and lace with a plunging décolletage and a butterfly bow in the back. Tied around her neck was a black velvet ribbon with her own diamond worth a million dollars. It was rumored that police guards were hired to secure the premises for Liz's grand entry.

Appearing without her husband, Prince Rainier III of Monaco, Princess Grace arrived solo to the Rothschilds' ball. To avoid the embarrassment of entering alone, Baron Alexis de Redé offered the princess his arm and escorted her through the front doors of the 110-year-old château. Grace looked every bit regal in her gold-dotted black chiffon gown by Yves Saint Laurent and diamond tiara.

Also opting for a dark gown was the Duchess of Windsor who, like the princess, was fending for herself that evening. She was overheard saying that the duke hadn't come because he was having trouble with his eyes, but she couldn't help but notice that his eyes never bothered him when he wanted to play golf. Flattered by all the attention, Baron de Redé was at the ready to escort the lone duchess. The duchess came in with her maid and a large Maison Givenchy dress box safely storing her midnight blue silk dress. In a separate room in the house, she changed into her gown before having her coiffure redone by Alexandre de Paris, who had set up shop in a room provided by the Rothschilds. There, Alexandre tended to the delicate tresses of his clients whom he had worked on earlier that day at his salon in Paris. The duchess's coiffure was pulled up into a chignon and embellished with a green ostrich plume that complemented her 60-carat pear-shaped diamond securely pinned to her shoulder.

Flying in from Rome were Dr. and Mrs. Andrea Dotti. Audrey, fully embracing the Italian culture, looked angelic in her all white netted gown by Valentino. The white dress was created exclusively for her in 1969, when she first moved to Rome. Made of white tulle, the full-length dress was covered in oriental pearls, porcelain beads, and small crystals. The high-neck collar and the cuffs on the sleeves were accentuated with organza ruffles and fashioned with pearls and beads, with a thick band of white silk taffeta wrapped around her waist. Her petal-like updo, created by the master Alexandre de Paris, was made of soft curls and adorned with white roses. Audrey had been sporting her new signature curls since having her hair permed earlier that year. Her famous eyes were emphasized by dark liner and thick false eyelashes, and for a touch of whimsy, she added a beauty mark near her left eye. She entered with white gloves but quickly removed them to light her cigarette. "Audrey looked very simple, very charming—like a little girl at a picnic,"[160] wrote Cecil Beaton for *Vogue* magazine. A Renaissance man, Cecil Beaton was hired

by *Vogue* to cover the gala for a photo essay in their January 15, 1972, issue.

Other notable guests included Andy Warhol, whose date, Jane Holzer, shocked everyone with her transparent dress. Countess Jacqueline de Ribes wore a pink satin and tulle gown, and Marisa Berenson, fashion model and granddaughter of Elsa Schiaparelli, was dressed as the Marchesa Luisa Casati in a Piero Tosi design, a curled red wig, and a massive headdress with black feathers and a butterfly ornament. "As soon as you arrived at Ferrières it was like going back in time, but more luxuriously with highly refined taste. The women wore dresses, bodices, big headdresses, tiaras, lots of jewelry. It was truly the era of Proust,"[161] Marisa reminisced about the lavish affair. Also in attendance were French actress and singer Jane Birkin, French musician Serge Gainsbourg, Princess Diane von Fürstenberg, surrealist artist Salvador Dalí, English fashion model Penelope Tree, French actress Capucine, worldrenowned pianist Arthur Rubinstein, Italian actress Elsa Martinelli, Princess Maria Pia, and her sister, the former Princess Maria Gabriella of Italy.

Dinner was intended for 9:30 P.M. but wasn't served until an hour later. Everyone made their way to the ballroom, which was arranged to look like a winter garden. Interior decorators Jean-François Daigre and Valerian Rybar had transformed the ballroom into a massive conservatory filled with thousands of tropical plants, flowers, and ferns that climbed up the built-in glass trellises. Suspended from above were crystal chandeliers flanked by green taffeta that covered the length of the thirty-foot ceiling. Everything was purple. The mauve tablecloths were decorated with a green floral display and a beautiful arrangement of orquídeas cattleya (cattleya orchids) in exquisite shades of purple. The orchids were Proust's character Odette Swann's favorite flower. Nestled in the blooming centerpieces was a mauve-colored fan

with the name of each individual table. The tables were named after characters from *Remembrance of Things Past*. The room was able to accommodate thirty-five tables with ten place settings per table. At Guy de Rothschild's table were Elizabeth Taylor, Princess Grace, and the Duchess of Windsor, and seated side by side at the baroness's table were Audrey Hepburn and Pierre Salinger. Keeping with the color of the night, the menus and place cards were written in violet ink. One hundred waiters dressed in red coats were at the dinner guests' beck and call. On the menu was "consommé Aurelie, mousse line de sole Mahenu, conned à la madrilene, salads Clarinda and soufflé place Agenor to eat and Château LaFite-Rothschild 1965, Moët et Chandon brut imperial 1962, and Château Yquem 1955 to drink."[162] Served on the side of the cold soufflés were Proustian madeleines.

ABOVE Audrey with the Rothschilds at the Longchamp Racecourse.

After dinner, an additional 250 partygoers arrived and congregated in the ballroom for dancing while a myriad of people retreated to the main salons to mingle. Princess Grace chose to blend into the background, putting on her prescription glasses and curling up on a sofa to observe the comings and goings. At 3:00 A.M. a buffet was given to revive the guests and keep them fueled until 6:00 A.M., when the party finally began to wane. In the early hours of the morning, chauffeured cars drove up the long pathway to Château de Ferrières to retrieve their worn-out passengers and return them to modern times.

The following year, on December 12, 1972, the Rothschilds once again sent out invitations to their annual ball at Château de Ferrières. This year's theme? *Diner de têtes surréalistes*, translated as "The Surrealist Ball." The theme was quite the departure from the Proust Bal; even the invitations (which were written backward) required a mirror to unearth their meaning. The dress code was printed as CRAVATE NOIRE—ROBE LONGUE (black tie—long dress), which seemed far less intricate than the period gowns that had been worn the year before. At least, one would think.

That evening at 9:00 P.M. guests made their way up the long driveway to Château de Ferrières. Contrary to the year prior, their current guest list was infinitely smaller in size; only 150 people were invited to the intimate affair. Rumors circulated that the noticeable downsizing was related to the Rothschilds' financial issues. The entrance to Château de Ferrières, like the year before, was pitch-dark, with only a hint of light gleaming from the candelabras carried by footmen dressed as cats. Everyone was outfitted in outlandish disguises, befitting of a Halloween extravaganza. The hospitable host, Marie-Hélène, wore a bejeweled golden stag head with antlers that towered several feet above her head. Her husband, the baron, elected for a more toned-down look, simply adorning a black fur hat with his matching black tux. Many of the arrivals embraced the over-the-top apparel and arrived dressed in disturbing getups inspired by popular surrealist artists.

Audrey's ensemble was in reference to one of her favorite artists, René Magritte. Audrey wore a Valentino red chiffon gown and fitted over her head was a wicker birdcage with fake white doves fastened to the bars. For convenience, the cage had a little door that could be opened when it was time to eat. Audrey was not alone in paying tribute to Magritte; men in bowler hats were often seen making their way throughout the party. The Rothschilds' affair could be considered a success by the number of faces camouflaged in face paint and bizarre headdresses. It was a miracle that guests were able to balance their absurd headpieces without falling over. All but one person dressed for the occasion; Salvador Dalí, who in fact *was* a surrealist painter, excluded himself from the dress code, simply saying, "I don't need a mask. My face is my mask."[163]

After Audrey's retirement from acting, her life became more insulated and these types of parties happened fewer and farther in between: "For many years, ever since I was a child, and all through my first marriage to Mel, I was always traveling around making films. So I wanted and needed rest. I hated the idea of leaving the children once they started school, and my husband must be near his clinic."[164] The occasional Hollywood friend, like Mr. and Mrs. David Niven or William Wyler, would stop in Rome to visit with the Dottis, but as Audrey admitted, "We don't have much of a social life. I never cared for that."[165] Audrey had been mentally preparing for this new juncture for some time, where her only obligation was to herself and her family. Signora Dotti had earned that much. ✶

# { 20 }
# Bloodline

After a nine-year hiatus, Audrey surprised audiences when she reappeared on the big screen in the 1976 film *Robin and Marian*, starring Sean Connery. Despite her lengthy withdrawal from the movie industry, Hollywood wasn't prepared to give up on Audrey just yet. Studios and directors continued to send the former leading lady scripts in hopes of her imminent return. But Audrey was content away from the limelight. She had chosen to make her life in Rome. Where many working actresses missed out on watching their children grow up, Audrey adopted a different approach. Her children were her greatest gift, and after suffering multiple miscarriages, she valued the preciousness of life. Having been raised by a withholding mother, Audrey wanted a better upbringing for her boys. It was the simple pleasures she appreciated most, like walking her sons to school, helping them with their homework, throwing birthday parties, and sitting down to dinner each night. Her routine at home seemed standard but, like with her first husband, Mel Ferrer, her marriage to Andrea was slowly deteriorating. Andrea was nine years Audrey's junior and a fan of the nightlife. Paparazzi would photograph him at nightclubs with women other than his wife. The tabloids printed photos of Andrea leaving clubs at two or three in the morning, questioning the solidity of the Dottis' marriage and Andrea's loyalty. Whether or not Audrey was in denial of her husband's flagrant extramarital activities, she was resolute about safeguarding her marriage from the media: "It's not pleasant for either of us when those pictures appear, of course it's not. We have words, just like any couple would. But we just have to cope with it and ignore it as best we can. I try not to think about it and I never like to discuss it with anyone else."[166]

Knowing her husband was unfaithful undoubtedly took its toll on Audrey's physical and mental health. But things were about to escalate—one evening in Rome in 1976, Andrea was assaulted on his way home from work. "I tell you, it's a very anguishing period in Rome," Audrey shared with Rex Reed in an interview for the New York premiere of *Robin and Marian*. "They're even kidnapping tourists for fifty dollars apiece, ransacking apartments and breaking into cars. There are so many different groups—some do it for political reasons, some for money, and others are just delinquents who do it for kicks. If you're a famous person, it's especially worrying, but I can't let fear dominate my life."[167] Audrey was concerned for the welfare of her sons. In an effort to protect her family, she moved back to Switzerland with Luca and Sean, while Andrea remained in Rome to be near his clinic. Audrey enrolled Luca at Lycée Francais, an elementary school in Tolochenaz, and Sean at Institut Le

Rosey, a boarding school in Rolle. "Now I shuttle back and forth between my husband and his work in Rome and the children in Switzerland," Audrey specified. "It's not an ideal way to live, but it seems the best thing to do for the moment."[168] It wasn't until the police cleared the event eighteen months later, claiming it was unrelated to ransom, that Audrey and Luca returned to Rome; Sean stayed in Switzerland until earning his diploma in 1978.

There was a lot of unrest at home, and the cumulation of her crumbling marriage and the political climate in Rome resulted in Audrey's welcomed homecoming to the silver screen. But securing Audrey for a movie was no easy task.

ABOVE LEFT Hubert and Audrey, wearing her ruby red hat, on their way to dinner at Maxim's. ABOVE RIGHT Audrey with Capucine and Hubert leaving L'Orangerie restaurant during her three-day work trip for *Bloodline*.

The biggest hurdle was just getting her to read the script, as described by director Terence Young: "First of all you spend a year or so convincing her to accept even the principle that she might make another movie in her life. Then you have to persuade her to read a script. Then you have to make her understand that it is a good script. Then you have to persuade her that she will not be totally destroying her son's life by spending six or eight weeks on a film set. After that, if you are really lucky, she might start talking about the costumes. More probably she'll just say she has to get back to her family and cooking the pasta for dinner, but thank you for thinking of her."[169]

However, due to her domestic circumstances, Audrey was open to the idea of acting again. Her *Wait Until Dark* director, Terence Young, sent her the script for the movie *Bloodline*, based on the book by Sidney Sheldon. The screenplay for *Bloodline* left little to be desired, but Audrey's contract secured her a $700,000 payday plus a percentage of profit. The role of Elizabeth Roffe (played by Audrey) was originally written for a twenty-three-year-old, but to accommodate Audrey's casting they modified the character's age to thirty-five—regardless of the actress's actual age, which was forty-nine at the time of filming in 1978. Audrey wasn't discouraged by the age amendment. In fact, she had a realistic perspective on aging: "Age? I don't worry about it. One worries about how one's life is, sure. I've got very good health. Whatever age you are, it's happiness that counts [ . . . ] I can't expect to be the leading lady all my life, that's why I'd be thrilled if people offer me character parts in the future. I won't resent it. Either you face up to it and say to yourself: you're not going to be 18 all your life. Or you're going to be in for a terrible shock when you see the wrinkles and the white hair!"[170]

*Bloodline* wasn't the comeback fans were hoping for, but it allowed Audrey to work close to home and still be near her children. She explained, "I did *Bloodline* because I had periods between locations where I could go home to Switzerland if Luca had a cold. Had *Bloodline* been a production that would have required four months on the other side of the earth, I would not have done it."[171]

Another benefit of *Bloodline* was the reunion of Audrey and Hubert de Givenchy. It had been twelve years since audiences had seen Audrey don one of Givenchy's couture creations on-screen. Both Audrey's and Hubert's styles had evolved since their last collaboration in the 1966 romantic comedy *How to Steal a Million*. Fashion had advanced since the midsixties, when clothes had reflected the space age movement and mod was all the rage. Now, silhouettes were more billowy and less structured, women were wearing pantsuits, and as for Audrey, she preferred a simple T-shirt and denim jeans for everyday wear. There was also her age to consider—she was approaching fifty and

wanted her style to reflect her maturity.

Before filming began in October of 1978, Audrey visited Hubert at his salon in Paris on avenue George V. Although Audrey had acquired a more sensible attire—"Mostly, I buy things in boutiques, and jeans are my way of life"[172]—her heart remained faithful to Hubert. "For me, Hubert is the best designer there is. He is more than a dressmaker; he is a personality maker. His are the only clothes in which I am myself."[173] Audrey's character, Elizabeth Roffe, was an heiress to a billion-dollar pharmaceutical empire and required a wardrobe that reflected her prominent status. Audrey, Hubert, and the movie's costume designer, Enrico Sabbatini, chose a selection of twenty-six pieces from Hubert's newest collections. Instead of contracting Givenchy for the movie, the studio bought the clothes off the rack and, as an added bonus, allowed Audrey to keep them for her own wardrobe. However, this exchange resulted in the exclusion of Givenchy's name in the end credits. Many of the items were separates consisting of wool blazers, knitted tops, silk cotton shirts, and slacks from Hubert's 1978 Givenchy Nouvelle Boutique line. "I think these are more important than the clothes I did for Audrey in *Sabrina*," Hubert said of his designs for *Bloodline*. "It's the *fashion* look. It's rhinestones, embroideries, veils, hats, gloves—all the elements of elegance. For the wedding scene in Sardinia, she wears a most beautiful blue dress with a veil and rhinestones. This time I make *all* the dresses for the film."[174] The knee-length, pale blue satin wedding dress with ruching at the neckline was worn during a wedding ceremony between Audrey's character and her costar, Ben Gazzara.

Hubert was not exaggerating; his designs signified a new era for Audrey, celebrating her age and womanly appeal. This was showcased in two evening ensembles. One was a black sleeveless lace dress embroidered with sequins and beads and worn with a black velvet blazer from Hubert's

Autumn Winter couture collection. The second, the pièce de résistance, was unlike anything Audrey had ever worn on- or off-screen. The floor-length evening dress had a bodice made of tulle netting beaded with rhinestones that barely concealed Audrey's chest and arms, with a generous slit up the side. Covering the remaining part of the dress was an asymmetrical design of black velvet that was draped over the front and back of the gown. Black velvet flowers were appliquéd on the tulle bodice with one singular flower strategically placed over Audrey's bosom. This, by far, was the most provocative dress Audrey had worn on camera, exceeding her flirtatious lace number from *How to Steal a Million*. She exuded a femininity and sophistication that could only come from life experience. Audrey wore the attention-grabbing dress at a dinner scene inside Maxim's, a well-known restaurant located on 3 rue Royale in Paris. Maxim's was a personal favorite of Audrey's, as she had dined there many times during her Parisian excursions. It was also the setting where Richard Avedon photographed her in 1959 for *Harper's Bazaar*. Audrey and Enrico procured the rest of Elizabeth's wardrobe at different boutiques in Paris and Rome.

Production for *Bloodline* began in October and wrapped in late December. Director Terence Young and his all-star cast, which included James Mason, Ben Gazzara, Romy Schneider, Omar Sharif, and Michelle Phillips, filmed the principal shots in Paris, New York City, London, Italy, Denmark, and West Germany. Rumors circulated about an affair between Audrey and Ben Gazzara, who was in the midst of a divorce. "She was unhappy in her marriage and hurting; I was unhappy in my marriage and hurting and we came together and we gave solace to each other and we fell in love but it was impossible,"[175] Ben admitted in his autobiography, *In the Moment: My Life*

*as an Actor*. The affair was strictly an on-set romance, which the two would resume when they filmed Peter Bogdanovich's *They All Laughed* in the spring and summer of 1980. According to Bogdanovich, Gazzara was infatuated with Audrey but emotionally unavailable. Their relationship was short-lived, leaving Audrey all the more lonesome.

In March of 1979, months after *Bloodline* had wrapped, Audrey returned to Paris for a nonstop three-day work trip to publicize the movie. She resided at the Four Seasons Hotel George V on 31 avenue George V in the Eighth Arrondissement of Paris. During her active seventy-two hours, she split her time between photo shoots with Italian photographer Sergio Strizzi, dress fittings at Givenchy, and dining at trendy Parisian joints like Maxim's and L'Orangerie. The publicity photos were shot by Strizzi at locations chosen by Audrey for a color story featured inside the pages of *LIFE* magazine's May 1979 issue. Audrey modeled her ravishing Givenchy designs from *Bloodline*, posing in front of Maxim's upstairs bar and standing on a banquette in Maxim's belle epoque dining room. Sitting outside at a quintessential Parisian bistro table, Audrey was all smiles at the famous café Les Deux Magots on Saint-Germain-des-Prés. Although these images were not used in *LIFE* magazine, Audrey modeled a chic silk cocktail dress with black-and-white polka dots and matching black-and-white hat from Givenchy's Spring 1979 haute couture collection. Wearing matching gray wool suits, Audrey was joined by Hubert on a rainy afternoon on Île Saint-Louis (a small island in the Seine River). However, the cold didn't hinder the atmosphere. With the help of his camera, Strizzi was able to capture sweet moments between the two friends. In the photograph featured in *LIFE* magazine, seated on a faded green park bench, smiling ear to ear, Audrey leans in as Hubert kisses the side of her face. The remaining color images were shot at the House of Givenchy. Audrey

OPPOSITE Audrey, photographed by Strizzi, wearing her black velvet gown at the upstairs bar inside Maxim's.

modeled a jazzy selection of new chapeaus from Givenchy's Spring collection, including a bright pink lacquered straw hat.

"It is difficult to analyze the special chemistry between the actress and designer or pinpoint who does the most for whom," Jill Gerston of the *Philadelphia Inquirer* said of the enduring team. "Their success goes deeper than a well-placed tuck or an extra pleat. No doubt it has something to do with their deep, longstanding friendship, which enables them to work together as a team— experimenting, adjusting, pooling ideas—rather than as simply 'dressmaker' and 'mannequin.' Together they enhance each other."[176] The sentiment behind Jill's words can be seen in the photographs taken by Strizzi. Audrey, still the

ABOVE Audrey and Hubert de Givenchy, photographed by Strizzi, on Île Saint-Louis in Paris.

pencil-thin girl from *Breakfast at Tiffany's*, now only wiser and more capable, looks just as exquisite as ever parading in Givenchy's timeless creations. The magic spark that brought them together some twenty-six years earlier hadn't diminished—if anything, it had only grown stronger.

During the same seventy-two-hour trip, Audrey visited Givenchy's atelier to have a strapless red chiffon evening gown with black dots tailored for an upcoming event. In April, Audrey would present a special award to her *War and Peace* director, King Vidor, at the 1979 Academy Awards at the Dorothy Chandler Pavilion in Los Angeles. On the night of the Oscars, wearing her red chiffon gown, Audrey walked onstage to an abounding applause. But first, during her week in Paris, Audrey wore her red-and-black dress at a victory party celebrating Guy de Rothschild's horse, Soleil Noir, who had taken home the top prize at the Grand Prix de

Paris, earning the baron a $20,000 payday.

On a separate evening, Audrey, Hubert, and actress Capucine dined together at Maxim's restaurant. Dressed in a black knitted Valentino cape and a Givenchy ruby-colored hat, Audrey found herself the target of paparazzi. Although her showbiz days were behind her, she still had trouble avoiding those pesky paparazzi. Hoping to have a little fun, and possibly disorient them, Audrey switched vehicles every time she entered and left an establishment. Yet, despite her best intentions, they still caught her and Hubert arriving in front of Maxim's. For all her efforts, it was still a decent attempt.

Over the next few years, Audrey would preoccupy herself with her family, the rare public appearance, and her next motion picture, *They All Laughed*, which featured Sean's acting debut. Bogdanovich admitted that Audrey's character, Angela Niotes, was loosely based on the actress's own life. However, by 1978, Audrey and Andrea had more or less separated. Her first marriage to Mel had left her stifled and yearning for fun. What she had found in Andrea was a man completely removed from the world of movies; here was an ambitious medical student who was lively, gregarious, and outgoing. But what friends had speculated in private would soon boil to the surface—the two were incompatible. Audrey was embarking on her forties at that point and ready to leave behind her years of traveling and parties for a more stable existence focused on building a family, but Andrea wasn't ready to settle down. He was still young and immature; it would be decades before he would grow into the man that Audrey needed.

After their separation, Andrea moved to an apartment directly across the alley from Audrey so the two could coparent Luca. Even though the marriage had caused her sorrow, Andrea and Audrey maintained an amicable relationship. Their main priority was their son, who had taken the separation hard. Their divorce was finalized in 1982, and it was amid production of *They All Laughed* in 1980 that Audrey met the handsome Dutch actor Robert Wolders. Despite their age gap (Rob was seven years younger), their relationship was built on a solid foundation. The two shared a similar background; both had been raised by Dutch parents and spent the war years in the Netherlands a mere ten miles apart.

Audrey's attraction to Rob was undeniable. In the infancy of their courtship, he would visit Audrey in Rome and make frequent trips to La Paisible. Soon, the two were inseparable. "I have a wonderful man in my life. I have *my Robert*. We have so much in common, he's so good to me, and he takes great care of me. It's a wonderful feeling to be able to not only love somebody, be loved, but to trust them,"[177] Audrey gushed in a 1989 interview with Barbara Walters. Rob was an attentive partner, never far from her side. As Audrey traveled the globe on behalf of UNICEF, Robert was there at every mission and televised interview, going as far as arranging all her travel accommodations and conducting mic checks before her speeches. When she was filming *Gardens of the World with Audrey Hepburn*, Rob was at every location, working diligently behind the scenes. Audrey was grateful for his companionship, exclaiming, "What a blessing he is because we do this together, I could never do this alone. Going around the world together. And he's just as passionate about children and UNICEF as I am."[178] Everyone saw how devoted Rob was to Audrey and her sons. In Rob, she found her soulmate. Although they would never marry (which Audrey considered even more romantic), the two would spend twelve doting years together until Audrey's death in 1993. On-screen, Audrey had fallen in love with Hollywood's most desirable actors, but after years of searching, she had finally found her real-life leading man, "her spiritual twin, the man she wanted to grow old with."[179] ✳

# { 21 }

# Oscars de la Mode & Gala SIDA à Paris

For decades, Paris had dominated the glamourous world of haute couture, and on Wednesday, October 23, 1985, the French fashion industry gathered together to celebrate the best of French fashion in their inaugural ceremony of *Oscars de la Mode*, "The Oscars of Fashion." The event was inspired by Hollywood's annual Academy Awards ceremony, but instead of a polished gold statue, the respective winners received headless busts made of Baum crystal. Fifteen hundred guests, wearing the chicest couture gowns and black ties, arrived at the Opéra Garnier for the live televised event that would air on French television from 10:00 P.M. to well past midnight and would later be replayed in the United States and Japan. The evening was given under the patronage of Jack Lang, the minister of culture, and sponsored by the Fédération Française de la Couture (French Federation of the Couture), du Prêt-à-Porter (Couture Ready-to-Wear) and des Couturiers et des Créateurs de Mode (High Fashion Creators), known as the Chambre Syndicale. The three big winners were chosen by fashion editors and journalists covering the Spring Summer collections in Paris. The ballots were cast at the tents in the Tuileries Gardens where forty-nine fashion houses showcased their latest designs over an eight-day period. A special jury, which included Hélène Rochas, Paloma Picasso, Andrée Putman, and Pierre Salinger, oversaw the selection of nominees.

Inside the Opéra Garnier, the grand marble staircase was adorned with red and pink flowers by decorator Jacques Bedat. Lining the staircase

OPPOSITE Audrey and Hubert arriving at the Oscars de la Mode at the Opéra Garnier. ABOVE Audrey arriving in Paris for the Oscars de la Mode ceremony.

were 150 models draped in custom-made red gowns created by the designers recognized that evening. French actress Catherine Deneuve wore a gray patterned dress designed by her date, Yves Saint Laurent. French designer Claude Montana, dressed in head-to-toe leather, escorted American actress and singer Cher, who wore an impressive spiked black wig with a Montana black knit full-length dress and exposed shoulders. Audrey Hepburn and Hubert de Givenchy arrived together and were met by great admiration from the crowd of esteemed designers and famous celebrities. Audrey looked incandescent in a multicolored evening gown by

Givenchy. The long-sleeved dress was made of sheer black tulle and embroidered with black paillettes and brightly colored silk appliqués in pink, yellow, red, purple, and green, which were cut like pieces of stained glass. Around her waist was a thick silk belt in shocking pink and accented with black rhinestones. Audrey accessorized her ensemble by adding a layered choker with faux gemstones that covered the entire length of her long neck. Pinned on the top of her tightly pulled bun was a pink-and-black floral hair ornament from Givenchy's 1985 Autumn Winter collection. Each guest was formally announced as they climbed the long staircase leading up to the main theater. The names—"Yves Saint Laurent avec Catherine Deneuve! Emanuel Ungaro avec Anouk Aimee! Givenchy avec Audrey Hepburn!"—were broadcasted over a cacophony of applause and an instrumental of Édith Piaf's "La vie en rose" triumphantly strumming in

ABOVE Catherine Deneuve, Yves Saint Laurent, Emanuel Ungaro, Anouk Aimee, Hubert de Givenchy, and Audrey at the Opéra Garnier. OPPOSITE Audrey, holding her Baum crystal statue, stands between the night's emcees Frédéric Mitterrand and Denise Fabre.

the background. Before the award show began, Jamaican model, singer, and actress Grace Jones wowed the arrivals with her rendition of "La vie en rose" performed in the foyer of the opera house.

Audrey and Hubert made their way through the doors of the theater, where they were joined by Audrey's companion, Robert Wolders. Amid the packed house, the elegant trio found their seats in the orchestra section, where Audrey was sandwiched between her two dates, Hubert and Robert. To Robert's right were French fashion designer Emanuel Ungaro, French actress Anouk Aimée, Italian fashion designer Valentino, and French actress Fanny Ardant. The Opéra Garnier was swarming with the elite of Parisian society, including French-Spanish jewelry designer Paloma Picasso, Pierre Bergé (the longtime business partner of Yves Saint Laurent), Danielle Mitterrand (the wife of the French President François Mitterrand), and French fashion couturier and the president of the Association of Couture Designers, Alix Grès. Madame Grès wore a black dress and red turban and sat prominently in the first row of the mezzanine.

All but one of the musical performances occurred in the foyer of the Paris Opera. Soprano Barbara Hendricks gave a meaningful performance on the main stage as she sang her aria from the opera *Manon*. The actual award ceremony didn't begin until midnight. The Fashion Oscars were hosted by television presenters Frédéric Mitterrand (the nephew of the president of France) and Denise Fabre. The two emcees read off cue cards and gave a clumsy presentation, often interrupting each other. The top winner of the evening was Tunisian designer Azzedine Alaïa, who took home two crystal busts for "Creator of the Year" and a special award selected by the jury that he shared with French designer, the "Queen of Knits," Sonia Rykiel. Alaïa, who was crippled by shyness, was so overcome by the announcement that he practically had to be carried onstage

by Grace Jones, who looked radiant in her fuchsia Alaïa hooded, lace-up gown. Alaïa was too bashful to give a speech and stood there as everyone lovingly fussed over him and applauded. Standing behind him were the models wearing their red designer-label gowns posed like Grecian goddesses on a staircase built on the stage.

The person who was met by the biggest applause of the evening was Audrey Hepburn. She received an award for her contribution to the French fashion industry through her personal style and movie costumes. The emcees listed off her repertoire of films, including *Sabrina*, *Love in the Afternoon*, and *Breakfast at Tiffany's*, at which point Audrey looked over at Hubert and smiled. At the mention of her name, "Madame Audrey Hepburn!," the crowd perked up and cheered with excitement. Audrey rose from her seat and kissed Hubert as she made her way toward the aisle. For a brief moment, she looked up at the

balconies and beamed with appreciation. The praise grew louder as Audrey approached the stage. She looked out over the audience, blew a kiss, and humbly bowed. Even the stationary models standing in the background generously clapped for their idol. Audrey, who was surprised by the special honor, addressed the room in French, "I am terribly happy, really delighted, but I don't understand very well. When you receive an Oscar it's about what you've done and I did absolutely nothing. For thirty years, as you said, I wore the dresses of my great Hubert, great in every possible way, for his beauty, for his talent and his friendship. Thank you."[180] Her eyes were flooded with affection. She looked toward Hubert and blew him one more kiss.

ABOVE Audrey with Robert Wolders, Baron Guy, and Baroness Marie-Hélène Rothschild at the Moulin Rouge, 1986. OPPOSITE Audrey and Robert at the Gala SIDA à Paris at Le Paradis Latin, 1985

Another winner that evening was Japanese designer Issey Miyake, who won for Best Foreign Designer, beating out Valentino, Yohji Yamamoto, and Comme des Garçons. The nominees for Best Spring Collection and Best Designer were Thierry Mugler, Sonia Rykiel, Anne-Marie Beretta, Jean Paul Gaultier, Kenzo, Angelo Tarlazzi, Karl Lagerfeld, Popy Moreni, Dorothee Bis and Jean-Charles de Castelbajac, and the winners were Claude Montana and Azzedine Alaïa. The jury also gave out special awards to John Fairchild, the publisher of *Women's Wear Daily*, and Hélène Lazareff, the founding editor of *Elle* magazine. Other special awards went to Pierre Cardin, Emanuel Ungaro, Courréges, and Yves Saint Laurent (who won for his "contribution to the history of fashion"). Homage was paid to the pioneers of couture: Balenciaga, Madame Grès, Chanel, and Christian Dior. One of the more touching moments was the presentation of workers from Dior's atelier. Dressed in their white smocks, the group of over one hundred people gathered on stage in tribute of the late Christian Dior.

Well after midnight, a candlelit supper was provided for six hundred in the foyer of the Paris Opera. The guests dined on crabmeat mousse, duck, and ice cream at tables covered in red tablecloths. The evening's festivities lasted well into the night, finally winding down at 3:00 A.M. It seemed that most attendees enjoyed the award ceremony, while some complained that there was too much focus on the celebrities and not the designers. Although many had hoped that *Oscars de la Mode* would become an annual tradition, the 1985 ceremony would be its first and final show.

The following month, on November 25, Audrey and Robert attended Gala SIDA à Paris, the first ever gala for the Fight Against AIDS, a charity dinner given to raise funds for AIDS research. The function was organized by actress Elizabeth Taylor and French singer Line Renaud, who created the Association of Artists Against AIDS in

1985. Liz Taylor had begun her crusade as an AIDS activist when her close friend and former costar, actor Rock Hudson, announced his diagnosis with the fatal disease; he sadly passed away in October of 1985. The month prior, in September, Liz had cofounded AmFAR (the American Foundation for AIDS Research) and raised millions of dollars in her pursuit to find a cure. The Fight Against AIDS gala cost $250 to attend and was held at the Le Paradis Latin, a famous cabaret in the Latin Quarter of Paris. Many notable names were in attendance including Jacques Chirac (the mayor of Paris); Marie-Hélène de Rothschild; French actress Françoise Fabian; French politician Simone Veil; French singers Dalida, Serge Lama, and Mireille Mathieu; and American performer Eartha Kitt, who performed a duet with Line Renaud singing Eartha's hit song, "C'est si bon." During the event, Line and Audrey conducted the raffle draw, French violinist Catherine Lara performed onstage, and

Jacques Chirac presented Liz Taylor with an award for her fearless efforts to mobilize the cause for AIDS research. Over the next seven years, Audrey would continue to offer her support to the fight against AIDS, joining Liz once again in Paris for a charity event at the Moulin Rouge in 1986 and in Basel, Switzerland, in June of 1991. Liz and Audrey had first met in the 1950s and remained friends over the course of forty years. On March 29, 1993, two months after Audrey's death, Elizabeth Taylor would accept the Jean Hersholt Humanitarian Award at the Academy Awards. In her speech, she would pay tribute to her friend and fellow activist: "I am so proud of the work that people in Hollywood have done to help so many others, like dearest, gentle Audrey [Hepburn]. And while she is, I know, in heaven, forever guarding her beloved children, I will remain here as rowdy an activist as I have to be and, God willing, for as long as I have to be."[181] ✳

# { 22 }

# L'Ordre des Arts et des Lettres

Being honored with the crystal bust by the committee for the Oscars de la Mode was not an unlikely occurrence for the extremely decorated actress. Thanks to the success of her first film, *Roman Holiday*, in 1953, Audrey became an overnight sensation, making an impressive mark during her first award season. She won the Oscar, Golden Globe, and BAFTA for Best Actress for her performance as the runaway princess. That same year she collected her first Tony Award for her onstage achievement in *Ondine* and in 1968 was given a Special Tony Award honoring her work in the theater. As early as 1952, Audrey won the Theatre World Awards for "Promising Personality" for her portrayal in *Gigi*. Over the next two decades, Audrey would receive four more Academy Award Best Actress nominations for her performances in *Sabrina*, *The Nun's Story*, *Breakfast at Tiffany's*, and *Wait Until Dark*. Despite losing out on a second Oscar, Audrey continued to win accolades abroad, earning two more British Academy Film Awards and (for three decades) holding the record for most wins at the David di Donatello Awards for Best Foreign Actress. Yet the statues themselves held little value for the accomplished actress. She never put too much importance in award shows or trophies; when it came to judging her art, her worst critic was herself.

OPPOSITE Audrey proudly wearing her *Commandeur* medallion.

Having come from a background in ballet, Audrey had never been trained in acting and every movement, expression, or instinct was self-taught and developed through years of practice and discipline.

After her retirement from the film industry, Audrey would continue to earn praise and recognition for her lifetime of work and charitable contributions. In 1992 she won a Screen Actors Guild Life Achievement Award and a BAFTA Lifetime Achievement Award. On December 11, 1992, only a month before her passing, Audrey was bestowed with the United States' Presidential Medal of Freedom, the nation's highest civilian honor. Sadly, Audrey was too ill to attend the ceremony, but President Bush still gave a touching speech in her absence: "Audrey Hepburn, whose acting career put her among our most talented artists but whose work with the International Children's Emergency Fund put her in our hearts."[182]

In March of 1993, at the 65th Academy Awards (two months after her passing) Audrey received the Jean Hersholt Humanitarian Award for her work with UNICEF. The award was presented by her *Roman Holiday* costar Gregory Peck and accepted on stage by her son Sean Ferrer, who shared these heartfelt words: "[My mother] believed every child has the right to health, to hope, to tenderness and to life. On her behalf, I dedicate this to the children of the world. Thank you."[183] Posthumously, she was lauded with a Primetime Emmy Award for *Gardens*

*of the World with Audrey Hepburn* and a Grammy Award for Best Spoken World Album for her narration on the album *Audrey Hepburn's Enchanted Tales*. Collectively, these awards entered Audrey into an elite group known as EGOT winners, individuals who have won the top four major awards in television, recording, film, and theatre, the Emmy, Grammy, Oscar, and Tony. Audrey earned her status as an EGOT winner in 1994, making her the fifth person ever to secure the prestigious title.

ABOVE LEFT Audrey with Hubert de Givenchy and Philippe De Villiers at the L'Ordre des Arts et des Lettres ceremony at the Palais Royal. ABOVE RIGHT Audrey with her fellow *Commandeur* recipient, Sean Connery. OPPOSITE TOP Audrey receiving her medallion from Philippe De Villiers. OPPOSITE BOTTOM Audrey standing with actress Jeanne Moreau, Philippe De Villiers, Sean Connery, and his wife, Micheline Roquebrune.

Although the physical awards weren't of much importance to Audrey, a handful of honors meant a great deal to her on a personal level, like the Ordre des Arts et des Lettres. In 1987, Audrey received the Commandeur de L'Ordre des Arts et des Lettres (Order of the Arts and the Letters) for her significant contributions furthering the arts in France and throughout the world. She was reunited with her *Robin and Marian* costar, Sean Connery, who was also presented with the distinguished order. The Order of the Arts and the Letters was established in 1957 by the French minister of culture. The order has three grades, the highest being the *Commandeur*, in which the recipients receive a medallion worn on a necklet. The second ranking, the *Officier*, entails a medallion on a ribbon with rosette worn on the left breast and for the *Chevalier*, a medallion on a ribbon worn on the left breast. Those anointed with an order are not required to be French citizens but have to be at least

thirty years of age, adhere to French civil law, and have made notable contributions to French culture in the arts and literary field.

On March 6, 1987, Audrey Hepburn and Sean Connery were decorated with the *Commandeur* at the Salon Jérôme inside the halls of the Palais-Royal, located at 204 rue Saint-Honoré in Paris. They were presented with the medallion by Philippe de Villiers, the Secrétaire d'État auprès du Ministre de la Culture (Secretary of State for Culture). Visibly overcome with emotion, a teary-eyed Audrey stood still as Villiers, with assistance, gingerly placed the green-and-white-striped ribbon around her neck. As the room broke out in applause, Audrey kissed Villiers on both cheeks and, in French, expressed her gratitude: "I'm very, very happy and very moved,

especially because it's been thirty-five years, at least, since your country and your great Colette gave me my first chance. I like to think that today she would be very proud of me. I thank you wholeheartedly."[184] It was a full circle moment for the fifty-eight-year-old actress. It seemed like only yesterday when a tenderfooted Audrey had arrived at the doorstep of Colette's apartment at the Palais-Royal. But her reaction to receiving this great honor was abundantly deeper; it was rooted in her childhood. World War II had robbed Audrey not only of her youth but of a proper education. Her schooling was halted when she was a barely a teen and her lack of formal education left her feeling inadequate, at times describing herself as "ignorant." For the French government to recognize her in a tradition steeped in cultural importance meant more to her spiritually than she was willing to convey in her speech. Addressing the press, Villiers congratulated the two actors for "having managed to escape the stereotypes despite their worldwide fame."[185] Even Connery, best known for his role as the dashing British secret agent James Bond, confessed, "I'm much more nervous and moved than I could have imagined."[186] Holding hands, Audrey and Connery posed for photographs in front of the crowd of photographers. Hubert de Givenchy and French actress Jeanne Moreau were both on hand to witness the momentous occasion. Jeanne congratulated both actors on their immense accomplishment and posed for photographs with Audrey, Connery, and Villiers.

The next day on March 7, Audrey and Connery arrived at the Palais des Congrès for the Twelfth Night of the César Awards organized by the Académie des Arts et Techniques du Cinéma (Academy of Cinema Arts and Techniques). The César Awards, a national film award founded by Georges Cravenne in 1976, is regarded as the French equivalent to the Oscars. Each year a new president is selected to head the evening's ceremony and on this occasion the committee had chosen Sean Connery. Audrey looked lovely in a Givenchy full-length strapless black silk gown under a white dotted short-sleeved velvet bolero jacket with a sequined pattern trim. Audrey was regarded as one of the most venerated women that night. She was invited to announce the winners for Best Actress and Best Actor, which were awarded to Sabine Azéma for *Mélo* and Daniel Auteuil for his performance in *Jean de Florette*. In an interview from 2021 with Laureen Aslangul, Auteuil remembers an awkward moment with Audrey when he accepted his César. Overwhelmed by the excitement, Auteuil accidentally stood on Audrey's foot when he approached her on stage. Yet, all was not ruined. Audrey barely noticed the misstep and Auteuil recovered in time to give his acceptance speech. After the show Audrey joined Connery and his wife, Micheline, for dinner, where the three sat for interviews to discuss their lives in movies and the evening's events.

One year later, in March of 1988, Audrey would return to Paris to pose for the top French photographer and creative director of *Elle France* magazine, Gilles Bensimon. Always faithful to her beloved Hubert de Givenchy, Audrey modeled pieces from Givenchy's 1988 Spring Summer collection including a black lace dress with black satin three-quarter-length bell-shaped sleeves with blush pink roses. Inside Gilles Bensimon Paris studio, Bensimon took a series of stunning black-and-white photographs for a feature in *Elle*'s May 1988 issue. At the time of its publication, it was rare to see Audrey editorialized in a fashion magazine. Her priorities had shifted since her cover girl days; she was at a point in her life where she was more focused on her humanitarian work with UNICEF (United Nations Children's Fund). Bensimon cites these photos as some of his favorite in his abiding career, feeling lucky to have photographed the luminary.

Over the next two years, Audrey would dive into her role as a UNICEF Goodwill Ambassador, traveling globally with one goal: to improve the lives of children everywhere. The same month that Audrey stood before Gilles Bensimon's camera, she participated in her first harrowing field mission to publicize the famine ravishing Ethiopia and killing its people. That same year, she visited Ecuador, Turkey, and Venezuela. Audrey wouldn't have a moment to spare. Between televised interviews and fundraising activities, Paris was momentarily put on hold. But in May of 1989, she would finally touch down in Paris to appear in interviews on French television shows in support of UNICEF. In the summer of 1990, Audrey would make a special trip to Paris for her newest project, a documentary called *Gardens of the World with Audrey Hepburn*. ✳

# { 23 }

# Gardens of the World and UNICEF

D ear rose, thy joy's undimmed, thy cup is ruby-rimmed, thy cup's heart nectar-brimmed."[187]

These are the lyrical words by poet Robert Browning recited by Audrey Hepburn in the opening scene from the television series *Gardens of the World*. The premiere episode, "Roses and Rose Gardens," shows Audrey, dressed in a pale pink Ralph Lauren suit, strolling through La Roseraie de L'Haÿ, a rose garden south of Paris in Val-de-Marne, France. The dulcet tones of "La fille aux cheveux de lin" by Claude Debussy accompany lingering shots of roses in shades of pink, pale yellow, crimson, and peach. Surrounded by rambling roses climbing up a pathway of arched trellises, Audrey bears a striking resemblance to the flourishing flowers that consume this French garden. "For thousands of years, man has expressed his love of nature through his gardens—and no flower has been so loved, renowned, and cultivated as the rose."[188]

*Gardens of the World with Audrey Hepburn* was an award-winning eight-part documentary series exploring more than fifty of the most charming and captivating gardens in Europe, Asia, and North America. The concept for *Gardens of the World* was derived from the mind of Janis Blackschleger in 1989, who said, "We actually spent over a year developing it, without a host—believing that the ideas and concepts had to work in their own right first."[189] After securing the primary garden editorial consultants, Penelope Hobhouse and Elvin McDonald, Janis, along with her producer, Stuart Crowner, and their team, was left with the pressing decision of whom to choose as their host. One thing she knew for certain, "we did not want the requisite television garden expert, but wanted someone who genuinely loved gardens."[190] Herein entered Audrey Hepburn. "We knew Audrey liked gardens. But talking about gardens also means talking about various cultures and peoples of the world. We wanted someone who is deeply interested in other cultures and feels and looks comfortable in that role, such as Audrey does."[191]

Audrey had formed an unremitting love for gardens since her days at a boarding school run by the Rigden sisters in Elham, Kent. After her parents' divorce, it was believed that Audrey's father

OPPOSITE Audrey at the French rose garden, La Roseraie de L'Haÿ, for *Gardens of the World with Audrey Hepburn*.

wanted her to remain on English soil whereas her mother would have preferred for her daughter to live in Holland. However, during the summer months, Audrey spent her break with the Butcher family at their home Orchard Cottage in Duck Street. Audrey remembered her summers fondly: "My mother couldn't afford an English nanny, and she wanted me to speak English, so she would send me every summer to stay with a family I absolutely adored."[192] The Butchers were like a foster family to Audrey; they provided her with a sense of warmth and affection that she was sorely deprived of at home. Mr. and Mrs. Butcher would teach her valuable lessons that she would carry throughout her life, later passing their guidance onto her own sons. Mr. Butcher, a coal miner, taught Audrey about canary birds and their ability to detect carbon monoxide in coal mines. From his wife, Mrs. Butcher, Audrey learned how to name and care for the different kinds of plants. It was also by way of the Butchers that Audrey formed a special attachment to terriers; in the 1980s, Audrey and Rob had a total

of five Jack Russells: Jacky, Jessy, Penny, Tappins, and Missy (and six if you include Piccirì, who looked the part but was a foundling whose breed was never confirmed).

Years later Audrey would understand the true nature of what it meant to maintain a garden. Having survived the terrors of World War II, the act of growing a garden, cultivating, and nurturing seedlings was more than a form of amusement. It meant survival, the resilience of spirit, and the promise of tomorrow. "My personal belief is that my mother thought, in some ways, that God was not only in churches and prayer, but also in the nature of wellness. So by stopping to see how each plant is doing was a form of compassion. We have to learn a lot from plants—they can suffer from winter wind and things like that, but they have the strength to repair themselves,"[193] Luca Dotti, Audrey's son, shared with the *Telegraph* in 2015.

Tending to the orchards at La Paisible was a spiritual practice for the self-professed amateur gardener. Yet, despite her modesty, Audrey was well versed in the art of pruning and planting. Her gardener of thirty years, Giovanni Orunesu, taught her how to care for the abundant flowers, vegetables, and fruit trees—cherries, apples, pears, and plums—that thrived on her land. "I am not a garden expert, but I am a garden lover," Audrey asserted in an interview from June of 1990. "And I think that is almost enough—to have a garden. I obviously do a lot of weeding, budding and clipping, all the things that are easy to do. I spend a lot of time in the garden. I spend a lot of time looking up at the sky to see what the weather is going to do to my flowers. And in the summer we have very wild storms, because we live not far from the lake. And the next day my corn is down, but I prop them up. And they stand up again. That is what is so extraordinary about plants. Their resilience. With a little help, they revive. Like with flowers, it's the same with children. With a little help, they can survive . . . they can stand up and live another day."[194]

When the program was first proposed, Audrey suggested that the documentary have a poetic element to it. "At first, I don't think I understood what she meant by 'poetic,'" Janis confessed. "But soon I understood—she meant a fusion of art, music, gardens, people, quiet, sky, light, and everything."[195] With the addition of Audrey's abstract imagery, *Gardens of the World* was set in motion. Production began in the spring of 1990. Audrey, Janis, Stuart, and the rest of the *Gardens of the World* team prepped for a tightly scheduled itinerary. They began their travels in Holland in late April, then the Dominican Republic for two days in early May, followed by a short stop in the United States at Mount Vernon in Virginia, before jetting off to Japan in mid-May, then Italy and France, landing at their final destination, England, in late June.

Audrey arrived in Paris in mid-June for a five-day shoot showcasing some of the most renowned gardens that France had to offer. While in town, she and Robert Wolders resided at the Hôtel Plaza

OPPOSITE Mrs. Butcher (on the left) and Audrey with her mother (to her right), Baroness Ella Van Heemstra, at the Butcher's garden in Elham circa 1937–39.
ABOVE TOP Audrey with the Butchers' terrier dog.
ABOVE BOTTOM Audrey in her garden at La Paisible, 1967.

Athénée. Her first stop, on June 11, was Claude Monet's Garden in Giverny, France, fifty miles northwest of Paris. "Perhaps in no flower garden in the world is there a freer and more exhilarating use of color than the one here in the French town of Giverny. Claude Monet, the father of impressionism, created this garden with a painter's eye,"[196] Audrey proclaims as she stands in the backdrop of some of Monet's most well-known paintings. She carefully navigates the colorful flower beds of delphiniums, dahlias, anemones, and roses that softly

lay at her feet. Monet had purchased the 247-acre lot in 1883 and converted three acres into flower gardens, transforming his property into a sanctuary of imagination and tranquility. However, on the day of filming at Giverny their experience wasn't so serene. While the crew set up their shots and the director gave Audrey her instructions, an overzealous gardener, who was waiting to spray insecticide, wasn't thrilled by the holdup. After the final take, the director called cut and the gardener, without warning, turned on the sprinklers and drenched the entire crew, including Audrey and two unsuspecting artists still holding their paintbrushes.

Two days later, on June 13, the team arrived at La Roseraie de L'Haÿ, where they spent the day

ABOVE Audrey in Monet's garden, Giverny, for *Gardens of the World*. OPPOSITE Audrey with Rob Wolders at the Château de Courances.

filming at the famous French rose garden originally begun by Jules Gravereaux in 1894. At the time of filming, the garden contained over thirty-two hundred varieties of roses. Audrey always had a particular fondness for the classic flower symbolic of beauty, love, and war. In 1991, Audrey was honored when a new hybrid tea rose was named after her. The Audrey Hepburn rose, bred by Jerry F. Towmey, was a lovely tint of light pink. "The rose named after Audrey is beautiful," Luca remembers, "because they are a deep pink in bud, but when they open up they become a softer pink and then almost white. My mother positively loved them so much as she grew them in her garden."[197]

The following day was dedicated to Château de Courances, a seventeenth-century French château in Courances, France, just thirty miles south of Paris. The word *Courances* comes from the expression *eaux courantes* (translated as "running waters"), which is attributed to the many natural springs that supply the small French village and feed the canals, moats, and cascades of Château de Courances. "Courances is representative of the principles of seventeenth-century French formal garden design introduced by André Le Nôtre—which were transformative in their time not only in France, but the world over. Which is why Courances was chosen specifically for Audrey—for how it avails of these principles and yet it has a very site specific grace, restraint, and interpretation,"[198] Janis revealed. Audrey's last filming location in Paris was at the Jardin du Luxembourg on June 15, 1990. This sanctuary set on sixty acres is located in the Sixth Arrondissement of Paris, between Saint-Germain-des-Prés and the Latin Quarter. In the series' final episode, "Public Gardens & Trees," Audrey tells of how "in one of the first great programs of urban renewal, trees were imported from the countryside to line the streets and squares of Paris,"[199] foundational to the verdant Paris we know today.

ABOVE Audrey on a UNICEF mission in Ethiopia, March 1988.

Jardin du Luxembourg was one of only two scenes that required a reshoot; a filming of Audrey reading from *The Diary of Anne Frank* in Paris was also later reshot at Mottisfont Abbey in England. Anne Frank was an immutable fixture in Audrey's life. Anne's story would continue to follow Audrey over the years—once in Switzerland in 1957 when Audrey was introduced to Anne's father, Otto Frank, who asked her to play the lead role in the 1959 movie *The Diary of Anne Frank*, and again in 1990 when she was joined onstage by composer and conductor Michael Tilson Thomas and the New World Symphony to read from *The Diary of Anne Frank* for a UNICEF (United Nations Children's Fund) benefit called *Concerts for Life: An American Tour for the World's Children.* "Anne Frank and I were born in the same year, lived in the same country, experienced the same war, except she was locked up and I was on the outside," Audrey read aloud. "[Reading her diary] was like reading my own experiences from her point of view. I was quite destroyed by it."[200]

"I know that for Audrey the making of *Gardens of the World* was not only a marvelous adventure, but also one of the most rewarding experiences of her life and career," Robert Wolders said in connection with HGTV's premiere telecasts of *Gardens of the Worlds*. "Coincidentally it came at a time when she had become deeply involved with her UNICEF work, which served to even further increase her awareness of the fragility of life and nature—of the need to nurture our children and then environment."[201] Audrey's involvement with both *Gardens of the World* and UNICEF employed the philosophy of leaving the world a little better than how you found it, a worldview Audrey had heeded since her childhood in the Netherlands. Having experienced the benefits of UNICEF firsthand as a child—"I can testify to what UNICEF means to children, because I was among those who received food and medical relief right after World War II"[202]—Audrey felt it was her duty to give back however possible. Now that her children, Sean and Luca, were grown and out of the house, Audrey had time to fully devote herself to her humanitarian work. Soon, she would take to the Parisian airwaves to inform the French media about her firsthand account of UNICEF's lifesaving operations.

On March 9, 1988, Audrey accepted the role of Special UNICEF Ambassador, and a year later she was appointed the role of Goodwill Ambassador. Her goal was to use her celebrity to raise awareness for the charitable organization as she traveled the world helping children in need. She would only accept $1 a year for her services. In March of 1988, Audrey accepted her first assignment: to visit drought-stricken Ethiopia, a country that had been overwhelmed by famine, malnutrition, and a high death rate. However, her efforts didn't end there; over the next five years Audrey visited Turkey, Ecuador, Guatemala, Honduras, El Salvador, Bangladesh, Thailand, Vietnam, Sudan, and Somalia. She appeared on international television and news programs speaking in English, Spanish, French, Italian, and Dutch, all languages Audrey spoke fluently.

In May of 1989, after returning from the Sudan, Audrey arrived in Paris to give televised interviews on behalf of UNICEF. On May 22, Audrey appeared as a special guest on the French TV show *Du côté de chez Fred* with host Frédéric Mitterrand. Fred asked, "So, Audrey, what is your mission at UNICEF?" to which she responded in French, "In fact, it's very simple. It's about going there, see, feel, return, and tell. Even if compassion in the world is enormous there are many people who don't know. That's why we (UNICEF) depend so much on you, the media, which is really essential for us, it's often a question of life and death. This was proven in Ethiopia for example, when a lot of people were dying and nobody knew about it, it is true of Sudan, where there was a long silence and nobody knew about

the civil war and what was happening there. And finally I am a witness, a witness for the children and for their needs."[203] Audrey would continue to pop up on French programs testifying to the devastating conditions she observed abroad. On November 13, 1990, she flew to Paris to promote the launch of UNICEF's newest issue in their book series, *Nous, les enfants*.

Audrey knew that her work with UNICEF had its limitations. She alone could not solve the problems that threatened these countries, but through her privilege as a celebrity she could lend her voice to an important cause. It was the same with *Gardens of the World*. Janis noted that Audrey wanted the series to be a testimonial to the environmental inheritance for future generations. In the companion book *Gardens of the World: The Art and Practice of Gardening*, Audrey states, "By looking at our world through its gardens today, we reaffirm the simple human capacity to create beauty on this earth. [ . . . ] Perhaps if we now take a closer look at our gardens we will better understand how to find a way to save our lovely earth. Have we not lost sight of our only source of life? Or have we at last awakened to the fragility of our beautiful planet?"[204]

*Gardens of the World with Audrey Hepburn* premiered nationally on PBS on January 24, 1993, only four days after Audrey's death. Before her passing, Audrey had the pleasure of watching the 1991 special that first aired on PBS, but she would never know the profound impact *Gardens of the World with Audrey Hepburn* would have on her fans worldwide. On Sunday, September 19, 1993, Audrey would posthumously win a Primetime Emmy award for Outstanding Individual Achievement, Informational Programming for her work on *Gardens of the World with Audrey Hepburn*. ✳

# { 24 }
# Givenchy's Fortieth Anniversary Retrospective

Since resigning from the world of motion pictures Audrey's life had undergone a pronounced transformation. The final movie Audrey agreed to was Steven Spielberg's 1989 romantic fantasy drama, *Always*. In it, Audrey played a spirit guide named Hap sent to help Richard Dreyfus's character after dying in a fatal plane crash. Considering there was a time when Audrey had filmed two movies per year, it was unimaginable to think that since 1967 she had made only five pictures. It was befitting that in her final performance she played an angel.

In the same year that *Always* premiered, Audrey was appointed the role of UNICEF Goodwill Ambassador where she worked tirelessly crusading for underprivileged children in impoverished countries. Her friend actress Leslie Caron said it best: "Her career can be split into two chapters. In the first part she received all the glory she could hope for, and in the second part she gave back, in spades, what she had received."[205] In 1989, at the age of sixty, Audrey was still reputed as one of the most beautiful and stylish women of the century, but as she grew older, her commitments had shifted. Now,

when she attended a function wearing a Givenchy design, rather than to promote her own work, it was in benefit of UNICEF or to show support to a friend in the industry.

In January of 1991, Audrey arrived in Paris from Geneva on the 7:15 morning flight to attend Givenchy's Spring Summer haute couture collection at the École des Beaux-Arts, showing promptly at 9:30 A.M. Audrey was dressed in a military-inspired chocolate brown coat with gold metal buttons from the Givenchy Nouvelle Boutique 1990/1991 Autumn Winter collection, and underneath she wore a crisp white Ralph Lauren cashmere sweater and charcoal gray slacks. From the airport, she rushed to the fashion show, was escorted to her reserved seat in the front row and watched in admiration as Hubert's colorful designs walked down the runway. "Givenchy's collection was filled with bright pastels splashed onto wisps of organza that floated over the body in short chemises, neatly tailored feminine dresses with dolman sleeves or swinging baby dolls with flyaway backs,"[206] wrote Katherine Betts of *Women's Wear Daily*. When a reporter asked if Audrey would wear the clothes, she teased, "*I did.*"[207] Shortly after the show, Audrey posed for photos with Hubert backstage and then again at Givenchy's workroom on avenue George V. "He made my first

haute couture dress, and he was my first haute couture friend,"[208] she told the press. While there she selected dresses for her upcoming UNICEF commitments and for several Hollywood affairs including the Film Society of Lincoln Center's *Gala Tribute to Audrey Hepburn*, which was to be given at Avery Fisher Hall that April in New York City.

Over the next several months, Audrey would juggle a busy schedule before returning to Paris in September for a fashion editorial to be featured in *Paris Match* magazine, highlighting Hubert's career and their long-standing friendship: a friendship that had withstood forty years, nine movies, countless fashion shows, and an unwavering devotion. The photos were taken by French photographer Jean-

Claude Sauer inside Hubert's Paris home, the Hôtel d'Orrouer, a *hôtel particulier* (a grand townhouse) located on the rue de Grenelle. The stately residence was the ideal setting for the elegant photo shoot showcasing designs selected by Audrey from Givenchy's 1991/1992 Autumn Winter collection. Hubert's creativity wasn't limited to just the runway. He had an affinity for architecture and interior design and owned three homes: the Hôtel d'Orrouer, his Parisian mansion; Le Jonchet, a manor in the French countryside; and Le Clos Fiorentina, a farmhouse in Saint-Jean-Cap-Ferrat, his Mediterranean retreat.

The Hôtel d'Orrouer was designed in 1732 by the architect Pierre Boscry for Marguerite-Paule de Grivel d'Orrouer, for whom the estate was named. The master of *le grand goût français* ("the great French taste"), Hubert's decor was an amalgamation of neoclassical and rococo styles with an emphasis on seventeenth- and eighteenth-century French fixtures, including his collection of Louis XIV and Louis XVI

ABOVE Audrey reclining in Givenchy's black satin gown with a semibolero bodice in his Green Salon. OPPOSITE Audrey donning her black velvet and tulle gown on the balcony of Givenchy's salon at the Hôtel d'Orrouer.

furnishings. Reclining on a green damask satin sofa in his Green Salon, Audrey was photographed wearing a Givenchy black satin gown with a semibolero effect bodice embroidered with black and gold paillettes, multicolored cabochons, and Rosalind coral. Behind her are two Boulle armoires, one known as the "Chariot of Apollo" produced from the atelier of André-Charles Boulle, Louis XIV's ébéniste (cabinetmaker). The six-legged cabinet of gilt-copper inlay and tortoise shell holds Hubert's collection of Renaissance Limoges enamels and beautifully offsets the gold sequins on Audrey's gown.

On the balcony of his salon overlooking the courtyard of iceberg roses and finely trimmed hedges, Audrey coyly glances over her shoulder. She is modeling a revealing evening gown of black velvet

and tulle, studded with black paillettes inspired by the marble cabochon floors in the entrance hall of Hubert's Paris abode. The front of the bodice (which is discreetly hidden from view) provides little coverage and is adorned with a black velvet bow fixed just below the exposed chest. Audrey looks statuesque as the sunlight pours down her back.

Hubert had a gift for making a piece of cloth into something beautiful, refined, but also wearable. His homes were no different; he had the same capability when designing a room. His grand salon with high ceilings were adorned with ornate rock crystal and gilt bronze chandeliers that looked beautiful against the white-and-gold boiserie (wooden paneling) by the French carver Nicolas Pineau. Decorated throughout the salon are Etienne Meunier armchairs, a castellans canape (a style of couch) covered in green silk velvet, with matching brass floor lamps and his acquisitions of rare artifacts of silver, silver-gilt, bronze, porcelain,

---

ABOVE Audrey and Hubert posing together in his Grand Salon. OPPOSITE Audrey with reporters at Givenchy's 40th Anniversary Retrospective.

crystal, and marble. His extensive collection of antiques are arranged in an inviting and intimate manner, creating an atmosphere where one could relax, laugh, and catch up with an old friend.

In a separate photo, standing tall at six feet three inches, Hubert towers over Audrey, who is dressed in Givenchy's red sleeveless short gown with an embroidered bolero jacket in red brocade silk. *Paris Match* magazine suggested, "Thanks to your films, Hubert de Givenchy has established himself in Hollywood and in America," to which Audrey replied, "That's not quite right. It is always difficult to define who started: the egg or the chicken. Hubert made all the dresses for my first films. It was he who gave me a look, a *genre*, a silhouette. It was he who, visually, made me what I have become."[209]

A month later, on October 24, 1991, Audrey honored her friend at a retrospective celebrating the fortieth anniversary of Givenchy. The exhibition was unveiled at the Palais Galleria from October to March and showcased 140 designs handpicked by the man of the hour. "They are all my favorites," Hubert affectionately said. "I made the selection myself, and it was difficult. I made my choice from 350 pieces. I wanted to show a mix of colors and styles so the show would look alive."[210] Many of the garments were lent by his famous clients including Audrey, who had ten outfits on display: some from *Breakfast at Tiffany's*, a replica of her Inez de Castro gown from *Sabrina*, and dresses she had worn in her personal life and in the pages of fashion magazines. One of the dresses displayed was a short sleeveless black crepe dress with black feathers from 1968, which Audrey had worn at a Rome nightclub with Andrea. Another was a strapless blue silk gown with lozenge patterns of gold, blue, yellow, and white beads with a tulip skirt and matching large sash, worn to the thirty-seventh British Academy Film Awards in 1984. Also exhibited was a strapless fondant pink silk crepe bias-cut dress from a 1966 *Vogue*

editorial. When Audrey stood before the displayed pink dress, she mused, "So simple." Next to her was Hubert's longtime companion, Philippe Venet, who nodded in agreement: "So simple: it's just a piece of material."[211] Nonetheless, the standout piece, due to its avant-garde nature, was a scarlet red strapless satin gown with matching red feathered boa and an intricate bodice made of feathers and embroidered with arabesques of lacquered plastic, sequins, and black bugle beads from Givenchy's Autumn Winter 1988/1989 collection. Audrey wore the modern-day *Gone with the Wind* ensemble to the Metropolitan Museum of Art for the 1988 Council of Fashion Designers of America Awards in January of 1989. "Look at them, they're glorious, aren't they?"[212] Audrey said of her friend's timeless creations.

The first to arrive at the event were Guy and Marie-Hélène de Rothschild, who had donated a few of Hélène's own Givenchy pieces for the exhibition. Next to enter was Audrey. Hubert guided his friends on a private tour of his designs, which included the ivory satin dress with embroidered flower bodice and matching coat Jackie Kennedy had worn on her official visit to Versailles in the summer of 1961. There was also the 1966 blue-and-white-striped organza evening sheath and coordinating scarf owned by the Duchess of Windsor, a design Audrey had once considered for *Two for the Road*. One dress that stood out from the others was a little white dress made of organza with embroidered lemon motif that Givenchy had made for Princess Caroline of Monaco in 1960 when she was three years old.

The museum was flush with nineteen hundred of Hubert's closest friends, colleagues, clients, and admirers. Among the guests was the reclusive couturier Yves Saint Laurent, who was accompanied by his friend and designer Loulou de la Falaise. Also in attendance were the designers Countess Jacqueline de Ribes, Oscar de la Renta, Claude Montana, Christian Lacroix, Jean Louis Sherrer and his daughter, Laetitia. There were

ABOVE TOP Audrey and Hubert backstage at his 1990/1991 Autumn Winter fashion show. ABOVE MIDDLE Audrey and Hubert in his workroom after Givenchy's Winter fashion show. ABOVE BOTTOM Robert, Audrey, Yves Saint Laurent, and Loulou de la Falaise at Givenchy's 40th Anniversary Retrospective.

people of nobility such as the Princess Elizabeth of Yugoslavia, Princess Sybil de Bourbon-Parma, and Princess Ferial of Egypt, who said of the exhibit, "It took my breath away, it was almost too much."[213] Many of Hubert's loyal clients, like Bunny Mellon, Lynn Wyatt, Ann Ford Johnson, and Mary Wells Lawrence, came to congratulate their couturier. Photographer Victor Skrebneski, whose photos of Audrey and Hubert were featured throughout the exhibit, was also in view and wrote the introduction for the book *Givenchy: 40 Years of Creation*, commemorating the fortieth anniversary.

"Every woman wants to look beautiful; at least I feel beautiful when I'm in his clothes," Audrey expressed to the many reporters who were clamoring for her attention. "And they give me great confidence. Which is very helpful when you're making a movie or have a difficult scene; at least you know you look right."[214] For the event, Audrey wore a short Givenchy cocktail dress of black organdy with long sleeves, an oval neckline, and a scoop back with an attached mantle. Her flower-shaped earrings were by Swarovski for Givenchy. "He was always lovely," Audrey said of Hubert. "He was always beautiful, he always worked with integrity; even when fashion became rather strange and odd at times, he stuck to his guns. He stuck to what he thought was beautiful and here's the proof, it's actual, you can wear it all today and I'm very proud of my friend."[215]

Hundreds of lit crystal candelabras draped with ivy lined the steps leading into the museum. Inside, candles were suspended between the Roman columns of the Palais Galliera and burned bright in a chandelier wrapped in ivy and garnished with pink and red flowers. Champagne and canapés were provided by French catering company Lenôtre. Topiaries of raw vegetables and dried fruits were tucked between platters of tiny sandwiches, fruit tarts, eclairs, and truffles on a three-tiered table with a red silk tablecloth. Behind the dangling candelabras were life-size photos of models wearing Givenchy's memorable clothes. "This is a very, very emotional night for me," Audrey said, "not just because of the beauty of the clothes but because of my unconditional love for him and his integrity."[216]

Janette Mahler, Hubert's secretary since the inception of Givenchy in 1952, expressed her devotion to her boss of four decades. "It has been forty years of happiness for me. Every day has been wonderful. And tomorrow will be the same. He will be there at 7:30, just as he always is. And I will be there, too. And it will be another wonderful day."[217] Though Hubert had sold his fashion house to French fashion conglomerate LVMH (Moët Hennessy Louis Vuitton) in 1988, he remained the head of Givenchy. In 1995 he would officially retire. His clothes and impeccable taste would have an unforgettable impression on the world of fashion, thanks to his friend and muse, Audrey Hepburn, who helped immortalize his clothing in her movies and fashion spreads.

Givenchy's retrospective would be one of Audrey's last appearances in Paris; Paris, the city that had launched her career forty years earlier when a spry twenty-two-year-old actress climbed the steps leading up to Colette's apartment at the Palais-Royal, nervous yet excited for the adventures that awaited her. Two years later, bounding with spirit, she would cross the English Channel to knock at the door of Hubert de Givenchy's workroom. There she would meet her fashion soulmate, a young designer bursting with talent. They would forge an infallible friendship that transcended clothes, a friendship that was built into their DNA. In Paris she would film seven movies, including *Funny Face*. Once an aspiring dancer, Audrey would live out her dreams of dancing with Fred Astaire along the Champs-Elysées to the tunes of Gershwin. Over time, Paris would become her home away from home, a place she could escape to when times were stressful. "Paris has brought me a lot of luck,"[218] Audrey once said, and it was true. She would form some of her happiest memories in the life-altering city. ✳

# { 25 }
# Au Revoir, Paris

Audrey's final visit to Paris was in October of 1992. Audrey had returned from a trip to Somalia in September and was making her rounds visiting television programs to discuss the desperate conditions she had witnessed on her latest UNICEF mission. She appeared on *F2 Le Journal 13H* and the French current affairs show *Repéres*. In her interview with Jean-Pierre Elkabbach she spoke of the "hell" she saw in Somalia, "I think that, in the end, I won't be able to overcome this trip. Like you say, to enter a food centre for children, to smell the death, seeing corpses being taken away, seeing the eyes of the children in their skeletal bodies . . . These tiny little faces . . . It's unbearable."[219] This mission would have a devastating effect on Audrey. During her trip in Somalia she began to feel a discomfort in her stomach. As the pain continued to increase, Rob and Sean checked her into Cedars-Sinai Medical Center in Los Angeles. On November 1, 1992, Audrey underwent surgery to have a malignant tumor removed from her colon. Still at the hospital, her family would learn that the cancer, which had originated in her appendix, had spread to her to stomach. Luca flew in from Rome to be at his mother's bedside. On December 9, Audrey would undergo her second surgery; the prognosis was terminal. Nothing more could be done.

Audrey would say her last goodbyes to her friends before returning home to Switzerland. Her final wish was to spend Christmas at La Paisible with her family. Hubert de Givenchy arranged for a private jet to fly her home because of her frail condition. "That last Christmas is one of the most wonderful recollections for me," Robert reminisced. "It was so important to her to have the boys and me together. We were able to sleep in the same bed until the day she died, and once we shut out the lights, we were in our own world and felt very peaceful. It was just us. I remember that voice in the dark saying, 'This is the happiest Christmas I've ever had.'"[220] On January 20, 1993, at 7:00 P.M., Audrey Hepburn passed away at her Swiss home surrounded by loved ones. She was sixty-three years old.

Very few were aware that Audrey had chosen Hubert to be the executor of her will—a decision she did not make lightly. "She needed not only a friend, not only someone devoid of economic interests, not only totally reliable and discreet, but most of all someone with an understanding of both the big picture and the humanity involved. Someone with authority that she could rely on,"[221] her son Luca shared. Having been burned in the past, Audrey kept a tight circle of friends: "Mum learned the hard way not to trust anyone, that history had a tendency to repeat itself. She made mistakes and misjudgments but always with a safety net intact that she slowly built throughout her life and career."[222] Hubert wasn't just her *couturier*; he was her confidant, her brother, her surrogate father, and a kindred spirit. Their love was delicately threaded into their friendship like the ageless creations he designed for her. On that somber day, on January 24, 1993, Hubert, along with Sean; Luca; Robert; Audrey's stepbrother Ian; and Audrey's trusted lawyer, George Müller,

wistfully carried Audrey's coffin from La Paisible to the nearby church in Tolochenaz. Friends and family would fly from all over to see her one last time. Her gravesite, located in the quiet Tolochenaz cemetery close to her house, was consumed by thousands of tulips, roses, and daisies: a fitting farewell for a woman who desired nothing more than to have a garden abundant in flowers.

Audrey's legacy would prove to be indelible. Her polished style and European beauty would become synonymous with the city that was forever linked to her heart. Watching her realize her greatest fantasies in Paris filled audiences with a sense of optimism and a yearning to escape from their everyday lives. Just her smile alone was the perfect palliative to cure any case of the *mean reds*. For Audrey, Paris was her playground, a place where dreams came true. Like her character in *Sabrina* said, "Oh, but Paris isn't for changing planes. It's for changing your outlook. For throwing open the windows and letting in . . . *la vie en rose*." And that's exactly what she did. Audrey let in *la vie en rose*. ✶

OPPOSITE AND ABOVE Audrey leaving Hubert's atelier on Avenue George V, in Paris October 1985.

# ACKNOWLEDGMENTS

FIRST AND FOREMOST, my eternal gratitude to Luca Dotti, who took a chance on a first-time author. Your friendship and guidance added a personal layer to this book that couldn't have come from any other source. I appreciate the candor you showed when discussing your mother's life and your parents' marriage. Your honesty offered insight to the text that would have otherwise been absent. Thank you for entrusting me with *Audrey Hepburn in Paris*. This was truly a once-in-a-lifetime experience.

To my dearest friend, Liza Petukhova: without your help, this book would have been unthinkable. The endless hours we spent scouring the internet for old newspapers, vintage magazines, books, and online archives are a true testament to your dedication and generosity. This is why you faithfully hold the title for Ultimate Audrey Detective. My appreciation knows no bounds.

To my "Kings of Fashion," Eduardo Sousa and Henry Wilkinson. Eduardo: your wealth of knowledge about fashion is on a cellular level that truly astounds me. Henry, you are undoubtedly the leading Givenchy aficionado and your own talents rival the Gentleman Couturier. I thank you both for sharing your years of research with me so that I could create a book flush with fashion.

When I first began writing the chapter on *Gardens of the World with Audrey Hepburn*, I had one measly article and a pit in my stomach. It wasn't until I reached out to Janis Blackschleger that the chapter bloomed into something great. Thank you, Janis. Because of your kindness and enthusiasm we were able to create something wonderful that honors the beautiful work you produced with Audrey.

To my team at HarperCollins, I'm forever grateful for your continued patience and warmth. To Jenna, Marta, and Lynne, it has been a true pleasure working with the three of you. Your optimism and precision were an invaluable asset to this project. To Jacqueline and Deb, thank you for working overtime to help me cross the finish line. And last but not least, to Liz, who was the force that got the ball rolling. To my wonderful team: your support and expertise made this book possible.

To Margreet Mateboer, Siiri Sainio, Caryl Anne Francia, Leendert de Jong and Abdul Mustabeen. Thank you for lending a hand when needed; your love of Audrey was a source of inspiration.

To my mother and sister, whose constant support and love provided me with the encouragement I needed to complete this book. You were with me throughout every event and were always there whenever I needed you most. Words cannot properly express my gratitude.

Most importantly, to each and every Audrey fan: I have had the great privilege of running my account Rare Audrey Hepburn for the better part of a decade. Throughout those years, I have been able to connect with hundreds of Audrey fans who have sent me messages regarding our timeless icon. I've had firsthand access into the minds of what Audrey fans admire most about her life and legacy. At every stage of this book, I have kept that information in the forefront of my mind. When I was developing the outline of this book and pouring over photos, I always asked myself, "What would Audrey fans appreciate the most?" It's because of your devotion that this book became a reality. Thank you.

# PHOTO CREDITS

# NOTES

1   Dominick Dunne, "Hepburn Heart," *Vanity Fair*, May 1991, 132.

2   Robert Phelps, *Belles Saisons: A Colette Scrapbook* (New York: Farrar, Straus and Giroux, 1978), 263.

3   Ian Woodward, "Audrey Hepburn Reluctantly Takes to the Stage," *Asbury Park Press*, October 9, 1984, C14.

4   Claudia Cassidy, "'Gigi,' Starring Audrey Hepburn, Opens Wednesday Night," *Chicago Sunday Tribune*, November 2, 1952, Part 7, Section 2, Page 1.

5   Picture caption in *Vogue*, November 1, 1951, 90.

6   Colette, Letter to Audrey Hepburn, 1951. Personal collection of the Audrey Hepburn Estate.

7   Brooks Atkinson, "'Gigi' Is Trivial and Old-Fashioned Although It May Be Witty in French," *Courier Journal*, November 26, 1951, 6.

8   Françoise Mohrt, *The Givenchy Style* (New York: Vendome Press, 1998), 57.

9   Ibid., 66.

10  Lucette Caron, "New, Easy Elegance in French Collections," *Hartford Courant Magazine*, March 9, 1952, 14.

11  Edith Head and Jane Kesner Admore, "'The Dress Doctor' Audrey Has Model Figure," *The Spokesman Review*, May 24, 1959, 4.

12  Ibid., 4.

13  Frank Caffey, Letter to Russell Holman, Production Notes, June 5, 1953, https://collections.new.oscars.org /Details/Archive/70080921.

14  Genevieve Buck, "Givenchy, Hepburn: Well Suited," *Chicago Tribune*, September 10, 1989, Section 5.

15  Amy Fine Collins, "When Hubert Met Audrey," *Vanity Fair*, December 1995, 170.

16  Ibid., 173.

17  Ibid., 170.

18  Ibid., 175.

19  Ibid.

20  Bernadine Morris, "Givenchy's Style Has the Timeless Touch," *The Sydney Morning Herald*, June 15, 1982, 9.

21  Mohrt, *The Givenchy Style*, 87.

22  Collins, "When Hubert Met Audrey," 181.

23  Mohrt, *The Givenchy Style*, 88.

24  "Audrey Hepburn spreekt in Parijs geruchten tegen," *De Telegraaf*, February 23, 1955, 2.

25  "An Actress and a Mannequin," *Sydney Morning Herald*, March 13, 1955, 68.

26  Bob Thomas, "Audrey Hepburn Returns to Make 'Funny Face,'" *Lancaster New Era*, March 8, 1956, 34.

27  Mark Nichols, "Audrey Hepburn Goes Back to the Bar," *Coronet Magazine*, November 1956, 45.

28  Mary W. Jones, "The Small, Private World of Audrey Hepburn," *Photoplay*, February 1957, Vol. 51, 95.

29  Nichols, "Audrey Hepburn Goes Back to the Bar," 45.

30  Ibid.

31  Carl Clement, "Look Where You're Going, Audrey!" *Photoplay*, June 1957, Vol. 51, 46.

32  Ibid.

33  Jack Schemeil, "Parisian Rain Shows No Regard for Soaring Hollywood Budget," *Times Colonist*, July 21, 1956, 4.

34  Bill Strutton, "Audrey and Astaire Dance Partners," *The Australian Women's Weekly*, October 3, 1956, 36.

35  Charles Higham, *Audrey: The Life of Audrey Hepburn* (New York: Macmillan, 1984), 98.

36  Edwin Miller, "Dancing in the Darkroom," *Seventeen Magazine*, March 1957, 122.

37  Stephen Silverman, *Dancing on the Ceiling: Stanley Donen and His Movies* (New York: Knopf, 1996), xii.

38  *Reflections on the Silver Screen*, Audrey Hepburn, April 26, 1990, United States.

39  Fred Astaire, Letter to Audrey Hepburn, circa February 1957, https://www.christies.com/en/lot/lot-6099976.

40  Ward Morehouse, "Actress' Work Leaves Her Homeless, Happy," *Fort Worth Star-Telegram*, September 9, 1957, 6.

41  Ibid.

42  "'Ha il genio dell' organizzazione' dice di Audrey Hepburn il marito," *Stampa Sera*, December 6, 1960, 10.

43  Strutton, "Audrey and Astaire Dance Partners," 36.

44  Arlene Dahl, "Audrey Hepburn Adopts New Page Boy Hair-Do," *Chicago Tribune*, December 10, 1956.

45  Nora W. Martin, "Pigtailed Audrey Hepburn May Set Another Coiffure Craze in Movie," *Lansing State Journal*, November 25, 1956, 57.

46  Bill Strutton, "Cooper and Hepburn Co-star in Romantic Comedy," *The Australian Women's Weekly*, November 28, 1956, 37.

47  Louella O. Parsons, "Yvonne de Carlo, Cable to Co-Star," *San Francisco Examiner*, December 13, 1956, Section 2, 3.

48  Angela Fox Dunn, "Always Hepburn," *The Gazette*, January 14, 1990, F-2.

49  Morehouse, "Actress' Work," 6.

50  Barry Paris, *Audrey Hepburn* (New York: Berkley, 1996), 332.

51  Harold Heffernan, "Audrey Hepburn's Pet Finds 'Dog's Life' Fine," *Indianapolis Star*, November 27, 1960, Section 8, 3.

52  Dunne, "Hepburn Heart," 132.

53  Aline Mosby, "Best Dressed Audrey Hepburn Gets Some Advice from Mate," *The Record*, September 19, 1962, 77.

54  Lydia Lane, "Paris Styles Please Audrey," *The Spokesman Review*, May 10, 1959, 17.

55  Ibid.

56  *Diana Vreeland: The Eye Has to Travel*, video documentary, Gloss Studio, 2011.

57  Nadeane Walker, "Audrey Hepburn, Husband View Chanel Fashion Showing in Paris," *Intelligencer Journal*, July 30, 1959, 8.

58  Ibid.

59  Ibid.

60  "Dior's Fall Fashions Hoist Hemlines Above Kneecap," *Daily Independent Journal*, July 30, 1959, 10.

61  Audrey Hepburn at "Council of Fashion Designers '88" event honoring Richard Avedon, New York, January 14, 1989.

62  Phyllis Lee Levin, "Fantasy Marks the Work of Fashion Photographer," *New York Times*, April 5, 1957, 39.

63  Ibid.

64  Richard Avedon, "Paris Pursuit," *Harper's Bazaar*, September 1959, 145.

65  Ibid., cover page.

66  Ibid., 149.

67  Ibid., 158–59.

68  Ibid., 153.

69  Ibid., 154.

70  Ibid.

71  Bob Thomas, "Grace Kelly Poor Photo Subject, Says Glamor Pro," *Petaluma Argus Courier*, April 25, 1956, 8.

72  "Audrey Hepburn: The Girl with the Eyes," *Interview*, August 1990, 101.

73  "The Cleo Look," *Sydney Morning Herald*, April 12, 1962, 7.

74  Jaubert, Sas, and Restin, "Albert et Paola (trés amoureux) ont régné une nuit sur le 'France,'" 10.

75  Henry Gris, "Audrey Hepburn Talks Frankly and Intimately," *Woman's Own Magazine*, January 10, 1965, 14.

76  Henk van der Meyden, "Voor het eerst geeft Audrey Hepburn een openhartig interview over haar persoon lijke leven," *De Telegraaf*, September 8, 1962, 21.

77  Higham, *Audrey*, 155.

78  "Audrey Hosts a Party in Paris," *Pittsburgh Post-Gazette*, July 17, 1962, 14.

79  J.M.C., "Vacances Parisiennes (et laborieuses) pour Audrey Hepburn," *Ciné Revue*, June 28, 1962.

80  Robert Alden, "Paris Premiere for 'Longest Day,'" *New York Times*, September 26, 1962, 32.

81  Henry Gris, "'My Fair Lady' Calls Audrey from the Paris She Loves," *Press and Sun Bulletin*, January 12, 1963, 9.

82  David Bianculli, "Tonight," *Daily News*, Aug 7, 2001, 65.

83  "Don't Follow Fashion . . . Let It Follow You," *Quad City Times*, January 19, 1964, 11.

84  Bernadine Morris, "Actress Has Influential Fashion Role," *New York Times*, December 14, 1963, 19.

85  Gloria Emerson, "Co-Stars Again: Audrey Hepburn and Givenchy," *New York Times*, September 8, 1965, 54.

86  Morris, "Actress Has Influential Fashion Role," 19.

87  Ibid.

88  "Madame La Lorette La Creatrice di celebri acconciature," *Confezione* N.42, July 1963, 17.

89  Ibid.

90  Michael Katz, "Audrey Och Cary Leker Charade," *VeckoRevyn*, Nr 14, 1963, 16.

91  Gris, "'My Fair Lady' Calls Audrey," 9.

92  Ibid.

93  Lee McInerney, "Audrey Hepburn Enchants Critics," *Pittsburgh Post Gazette*, December 16, 1963, 22.

94  Ibid.

95  Edith Lindeman, "Miss Hepburn Charms in Table-Hopping Role," *Richmond Times Dispatch*, December 14, 1963, 31.

96  John L. Scott, "Hollywood Calendar: Bergen Throws," *Los Angeles Times*, December 2, 1962, 6.

97  Gris, "'My Fair Lady' Calls Audrey," 9.

98  Kate Cameron, "Cary Grant Was in Town and Left us a Picture for Christmas," *Daily News*, November 17, 1963, C24.

99  Hedda Hopper, "Hollywood," *Daily News*, September 23, 1963, 38.

100  Silverman, *Dancing on the Ceiling*, xiv.

101  Ibid.

102  Paris, *Audrey Hepburn*, 188.

103  Silverman, *Dancing on the Ceiling*, xiv.

104  "All I Want Next Christmas Is Another Picture with Audrey," *Movie Life Yearbook #34*, 1963, 64.

105  Eleanor Dwight, *Diana Vreeland: An Illustrated Biography* (New York: HarperCollins, 2002), 129.

106  Diana Vreeland, Letter to Audrey Hepburn, August 10, 1984.

107  Dwight, *Diana Vreeland: An Illustrated Biography*, 187.

108  "The Givenchy Idea," *Vogue*, April 15, 1963, 64.

109 Ibid.

110 Ibid.

111 Laurena Pringle, "Think Christmas Now," *Detroit Free Press*, November 13, 1960, 14-B.

112 Salvatore Gervasi, *Audrey Hepburn—Hubert de Givenchy. Une élégante amitié* (Lausanne: Favre, 2017), 25.

113 *Vogue*, June 1, 1963, advertisement.

114 Diana Vreeland, Letter to Audrey Hepburn, September 3, 1971.

115 "The Givenchy Idea," *Vogue*, 64.

116 Mary Blume, "Movie Keeps Audrey Busy," *The Austin Statesman*, September 14, 1965, A24.

117 "Famous Hairstyles Have Turned Heads," *The Montgomery Advertiser*, March 27, 1983, 7C.

118 Hedda Hopper, "'Fair Lady' Premiere a Star-Filled Night," *The Hartford Courant*, November 5, 1964, 22.

119 Sheila Graham, "Audrey's Film Based on Experience," *Orlando Evening Star*, December 9, 1965, 16-D.

120 Claude Berthod, "Audrey Hepburn," *Cosmopolitan*, October 1966, Vol. 161, 82.

121 Gloria Emerson, "Co-Stars Again: Audrey Hepburn and Givenchy," *New York Times*, September 8, 1965, 54.

122 Claude Berthod, "Audrey Hepburn," *Cosmopolitan*, October 1966, Vol. 161, 82.

123 Stephanie Mansfield, "Audrey Hepburn," *The Morning Call*, August 11, 1985, F3.

124 Hedda Hopper, "Tony Bill to Portray Oswald," *Detroit Free Press*, January 11, 1966, 9.

125 "How to Steal a Million," *Screen Stories*, September 1966, 53.

126 Ibid.

127 "New Girl on the Beauty Scene: Audrey Hepburn with the Coupe Infante '66," *Vogue*, August 15, 1965, 113.

128 Emerson, "Co-Stars Again," 54.

129 Ibid.

130 "The Wyckoff Shopper," *The Pocono Record*, Aug 31, 1966, 6.

131 Drusilla Beyfus, "Inside Audrey's World by Givenchy," *The Sunday Telegraph*, July 23, 2015, 27.

132 "What You Can Learn From A Great Makeup Artist," Vogue, November 1, 1972, 152.

133 Berthod, "Audrey Hepburn," 82.

134 Peggy Massin, "A Natural Look," *Baltimore Sun*, January 6, 1966, B6.

135 Violette Leduc, "Steal—Scening with Hepburn & O'Toole," *Vogue*, April 1, 1966, 173.

136 Terence Pepper, "Always Audrey," (Iconic Images and ACC Art Books 2019), 154.

137 Marjory Adams, "Teaming Elfin Audrey, Sexy O'Toole, Is Genius," *Boston Globe*, August 25, 1966, 47.

138 Peter Thomson, "Donen Examines Modern Marriage in New Film," *Fort Lauderdale News*, August 21, 1966, 18C.

139 "Look at Audrey Hepburn Now!," *Ladies Home Journal*, January 1967, 110.

140 Florabel Muir, "Audrey Hepburn Is Changing Image with Movie on Affair," *San Antonio Express*, July 17, 1966, B-H.

141 "Look at Audrey Hepburn Now!," 110.

142 Ibid.

143 David Stone, "My Husband Mel," *Everybody's Weekly*, March 10, 1956, 15.

144 "Look at Audrey Hepburn Now!," 110.

145 Higham, *Audrey*,180–81.

146 Muir, "Audrey Hepburn Is Changing Image," B-H.

147 "Look at Audrey Hepburn Now!," 110.

148 Ibid.

149 Ibid.

150 Ibid.

151 Ibid.

152 Bernadine Morris, "Ken Scott Gilds the Lily: He Adds Beads and Sequins to Flower Prints," *New York Times*, June 3, 1966, 63.

153 "Look at Audrey Hepburn Now!," 110.

154 Ibid.

155 Dorothy Manners, "Sizzling Words from Audrey," *San Francisco Examiner*, Jun 10, 1968, 34.

156 Ibid.

157 Henry Gris, "Audrey Hepburn Tracked Down: Her First New Interview," *Detroit Free Press*, Aug 29, 1971, 18.

158 Ibid.

159 Ibid.

160 Cecil Beaton, "Remembrance of Things Proust," *Vogue*, January 15, 1972, 18.

161 Raquel Fernández Sobrín, "Le Pal Proust," *Suit Magazine*, December 30, 2021, https://suitmagazine.net/le-bal-proust-anniversary/.

162 Suzy Knickerbocker, "Revels at the Rothschilds,'" *Daily News*, December 5, 1971, 10.

163 "In the Rothschild Manner, a Simple Dinner for 150 Close Friends," *New York Times*, December 17, 1972, 70.

164 Rex Reed, "Rex Reed Profiles Audrey Hepburn," Devault-Graves Digital Editions, October 31, 2014, 67.

165 Gris, "Audrey Hepburn Tracked Down," 19.

166 William Otterburn-Hall, "Audrey Hepburn Stars as a Vulnerable Victim," *San Francisco Examiner*, June 24, 1979, 17.

167 Reed, "Rex Reed Profiles Audrey Hepburn," 67.

168 Ibid.

169 Sheridan Morley, *Audrey Hepburn* (London: Pavilion Books Ltd., 1993), 103.

170 Otterburn-Hall, "Audrey Hepburn Stars as a Vulnerable Victim," 17.

171 Andre Leon Talley, "The Simple Style of Audrey Hepburn," *The Times Leader*, April 12, 1979, 6B.

172 Jill Gerston, "He Designs Them, She Wears Them, and All Hail Them," *Philadelphia Inquirer*, July 8, 1979, 4G.

173 Ibid.

174 Marylou Luther, "Audrey's Back and Givenchy's Got Her," *Los Angeles Times*, November 17, 1978, 2.

175 Ben Gazzara, *In the Moment: My Life as an Actor* (Boston: Da Capo Press, 2005).

176 Gerston, "He Designs Them," 4G.

177 *The Barbara Walters Summer Special* (TV Special), presenter Barbara Walters, March 29, 1989.

178 Sunday Sunday (TV Series), presenter Gloria Hunniford, November 13, 1988.

179 J. D. Podolsky, "Life with Audrey," *People*, October 31, 1994, 104.

180 Audrey Hepburn at the Oscar de la Mode Ceremony, Paris, France, October 23, 1985. youtu.be/tyOb5jCfHMg.

181 Elizabeth Taylor at the 65th Academy Awards, Los Angeles, California, March 29, 1993.

182 President George H. W. Bush at the Presidential Medal of Freedom Ceremony, Washington, DC, December 11, 1992.

183 Sean Hepburn Ferrer at the 65th Academy Awards, Los Angeles, California, March 29, 1993.

184 Audrey Hepburn at the Ordre des Arts et des Lettres Ceremony, Paris France, March 6, 1987.

185 "Connery, Audrey Hepburn Honor," *Los Angeles Times*, March 6, 1987, 1.

186 Sean Connery at the Ordre des Arts et des Lettres Ceremony, Paris France, March 6, 1987.

187 *Gardens of the World with Audrey Hepburn*, Perennial Productions, January 21, 1993.

188 Ibid.

189 Janis Blackschleger, Email to author, April 28, 2022.

190 Ibid.

191 Yoshiko Kasuga, "オードリー・ヘプバーン 花は現代の癒し," *BiseS Magazine*, No. 15, December 01, 2001.

192 Dunne, "Hepburn Heart," 132.

193 Miranda Evans, "Memories of My Mother, Audrey Hepburn the Gardener," *The Telegraph*, September 15, 2015, https://www.telegraph.co.uk/gardening /gardens-to-visit/memories-of-my-mother-as-a-gardener-audrey-hepburn-by-luca-dotti/.

194 *Gardens of the World with Audrey Hepburn Special Tribute Edition*, Perennial Productions, 2006.

195 Kasuga, "オードリー・ヘプバーン「花は現代の癒し」"

196 *Gardens of the World with Audrey Hepburn*, Perennial Productions, January 21, 1993.

197 Evans, "Memories of My Mother."

198 Janis Blackschleger, Email to author, August 23, 2022.

199 *Gardens of the World with Audrey Hepburn*, Perennial Productions, January 21, 1993.

200 Sean Hepburn Ferrer, *Audrey Hepburn, An Elegant Spirit* (New York: Atria Publishing Group, 2003).

201 Robert Wolders, HGTV's unseen footage of *Gardens of the World: Tropical Gardens & Japanese Gardens*, aired March 27, 1996.

202 Patricia McCormack, "Hepburn's Mission of Love," *Press Tribune*, March 25, 1988, A-12.

203 Audrey Hepburn on "Du Côté De Chez Fred," Host Frédéric Mitterrand, May 22, 1989, France.

204 Penelope Hobhouse and Elvin McDonald, eds, foreword by Audrey Hepburn, *Gardens of the World: The Art and Practice of Gardening* (New York: Macmillan, 1991).

205 Paris, *Audrey Hepburn*, 332.

206 Katherine Betts, "The Designer Shows Go On," *Philadelphia Inquirer*, February 3, 1991, 4-I.

207 Bernadine Morris, "In Paris, a Style Break from War," *New York Times*, January 29, 1991, B6.

208 Gladys Perint Palmer, "Givenchy Has Spun Fashion Magic for 40 Years," *San Francisco Examiner*, February 10, 1991, E-3.

209 "Audrey Hepburn Star Fidele," Paris Match, October 17, 1991, 102.

210 Bernadine Morris, "Givenchy, Once and Forever," *New York Times*, October 27, 1991, 46.

211 Ibid.

212 Genevieve Buck, "Picture Perfect Best Describes Givenchy Gala," *Chicago Tribune*, October 22, 1991, 22.

213 Ibid.

214 Audrey Hepburn at the Hubert de Givenchy Retrospective, October 24, 1991, https://youtu.be/2AM6v3PQea8.

215 Ibid.

216 Buck, "Picture Perfect Best Describes Givenchy Gala," 22.

217 Ibid.

218 Audrey Hepburn interview with Pros Verbruggen for *Premiere Magazine*, October 16, 1959, https://youtu .be/2Xbvb6W98iU.

219 Audrey Hepburn interviewed by Jean-Pierre Elkabbach for *Repéres*, October 22, 1992, https://youtu .be/_hP1KXdu2bA.

220 Paris, *Audrey Hepburn*, 365.

221 Luca Dotti, Email with author, June 15, 2022.

222 Ibid.

MEGHAN FRIEDLANDER is a lifelong Audrey Hepburn fan. She began her popular website Rare Audrey Hepburn in 2010 with one mission: to share rare and unseen photos of the celebrated actress. In the last decade, Rare Audrey Hepburn has become the number one online source for Audrey Hepburn and has expanded to all social media platforms including Instagram, YouTube, and TikTok. *Audrey Hepburn in Paris* is Friedlander's first book. She resides in California.

HarperCollins books may be purchased for educational, business, or sales promotional use. For information please email the Special Markets Department at SPsales@harpercollins.com.

FIRST EDITION

Design by Sarah Gifford

Library of Congress Control Number: 2022950440
ISBN 978-0-06-313552-9

24 25 26 27 28 IMG 10 9 8 7 6 5 4 3 2 1